Attuned Exercise

Reclaiming movement from shame, hustle, and perfectionism and building a deeper, more sustainable relationship with your body

WRITTEN BY

Martha Munroe

LiveLife**Happy**
Publishing

Published and Distributed in Canada by Live Life Happy Publishing.
www.livelifehappypublishing.com

Library of Congress Cataloging-in-Publication Data

Martha Munroe

Attuned Exercise

Health, Fitness & Dieting > Exercise & Fitness > Injury Prevention & Rehabilitation

Health, Fitness & Dieting > Mental Health > Happiness / Self-Esteem

Self-Help > Eating Disorders & Body Image

ISBN: ISBN: 978-1-998724-28-4 Papback Book

ISBN: 978-1-998724-29-1 Electronic Book

Cover Design: Martha Munroe

For more information, or to book an event, contact :
www.AttunedExercise.com | www.MarthaMunroe.com

Live Life Happy Publishing

PUBLISHER'S NOTE & AUTHOR DISCLAIMER

A book for anyone who has craved
a more meaningful relationship with their body,
with movement, and with the world

TABLE OF CONTENTS

PART THREE: Returning to the body
Reconnecting with a body that's been a battleground

PART FOUR: Practicing what's possible
Embodying attunement

Introduction

Hello!

I'm so glad you're here. If you're reading this, I'm going to guess a few things are true.

You *want* to exercise, or at least, you wish you wanted to. You know it helps with stress, mental health, energy, sleep, and a hundred other things. You've probably tried, maybe more times than you can count, and maybe, like so many people, you've ended up back in the same place: frustrated, ashamed, confused about why it never seems to stick.

You're not lazy. You're not defective. And you're definitely not alone.

The most common narratives about exercise often have very little to do with how sustainable change actually happens, especially for people with complex relationships to their bodies, fluctuating energy, or difficult past experiences. The predominant message has been: push harder, fix yourself, and don't stop until you get "results." It's a setup for burnout and shame (which immediately saps whatever motivational energy you had). Sound familiar?

This book offers something different. At its core, it's not about how to "optimize" your workouts, nor is it about how to 'finally get your act together'. It's about changing your relationship with movement and your body entirely. From something that feels like punishment, pressure, or perfectionism, into something that feels more like a conversation. A connection. A collaboration between you and your body.

If you've struggled to make exercise a consistent, energy-giving part of your life, you are not a failure.

You've likely been shown a narrow (or even harmful) version of what fitness *should* look like, one that disconnects you from your body rather than helping you inhabit it more fully.

You may have a tangled history of body image, diet culture, injury, or exhaustion. You may carry fear, frustration, or a deep sense of defeat. But that's not the end of the story. It's the beginning of a new one - one rooted in attunement, not control.

A little about me

I wasn't always someone who "loved to move." As a kid, I was more into picking dandelions in the outfield than playing sports. But I was curious about physical culture and the promises of the gym. When I got my first job at a gym (working the front desk at age 18), I stepped into a place that offered both empowerment and pressure. I felt stronger, more capable *and* also increasingly aware of how my body was being watched, measured, and compared.

This tension stayed with me for years: the real joy of feeling powerful in my body, tangled up with beliefs that I needed to *look* a certain way to be worthy or accepted.

Eventually, I became a personal trainer, partly because it sounded more interesting than working retail, and partly because I hoped it might somehow mysteriously give me the kind of "ideal body" I saw in magazines (something common to many pursuing the career who then bring that baggage to the role). Over time, I trained hundreds of clients in gyms, parks, and corporate wellness programs. I taught everything from boot-camps to Pilates to weightlifting, always jumping into the next certification, always trying to figure out what *actually* helped people stay consistent, engaged, and enjoying fitness.

After some time, I kept noticing: The clients who exercised to shrink or fix themselves, who were motivated by guilt, shame, or aesthetics, often burned out or struggled with motivation. But the ones who moved their bodies for other reasons, to feel better, to have more energy, to connect with others, tended to stick with it. Their *relationship with movement* had less friction. More ease somehow. Maybe more meaning?

I was still figuring out the language for what I was observing and trying different approaches with clients until the massive transition period when I became a parent. After a physically and emotionally difficult delivery, my body felt unfamiliar, even broken. I didn't know how (or if) I'd return to the physical life and work I loved. That experience was a springboard for me to get really curious, not just about what was happening physically, but psychologically and philosophically as well.

In seeking answers, I dove into postnatal movement research, trauma-aware approaches, and anti-diet work developing a model of 'fitness mindset' and how the beliefs we have about exercise can interrupt the benefits we glean. I then decided to pursue graduate studies in positive psychology and coaching psychology, where I studied the science of wellbeing, growth, and what actually supports long-term change. All the while with my eye on exercise, the body and wellbeing. Along the way, I discovered the field of **positive embodiment,** which offered words for the dynamics I'd been witnessing but didn't know had been studied: that how we *relate* to our bodies is just as important as what we do with them. This was the foundation of the research work I became involved in and it also became the foundation for this book.

Because, for all the talk about what kind of exercise is "best," we rarely ask *what kind of relationship* we're cultivating with movement, and with ourselves in the process.

A little about where we're going and how we'll get there:

Fitness as usual asks us to think of our body as an object somehow separate from us. It becomes something we act upon, attempt to seek mastery over, and disconnect from, sacrificing our in-the-moment feelings for some imagined future ideal. What we're aiming to do is explore a fundamentally new relationship to the body, with attunement and connection at the centre. Where we ask better questions about where we're hoping to go and understand that our body is something we *are* not something we *have*. Where we acknowledge that this journey is a life-long one, and that we can stop wasting our time, energy, money, and spirit in thinking our body is a problem and we are a failure because of it. We're going to explore how we got here and the things that have gotten in our way, and start to envision and explore a new path forward where exercise can not only be a positive in our lives but actually be a vehicle for greater attunement and embodiment, a tangible experience of a growth mindset in action, and a felt-sense of self-efficacy and self-compassion. The hope is that the information shared is both super practical and deeper than just another how-to.

We'll begin by clearing out the noise: the myths, the shame, the hustle culture that's shaped our understanding of exercise and movement. Then we'll build a new internal compass: one rooted in self-compassion, embodiment, and motivation that actually lasts. From there, we'll return to the body, not as an object to improve, but as a place to live from. Finally, we'll ground these ideas in practice, exploring how to move forward with flexibility, sustainability, and trust in your own inner wisdom.

Let's dive in!

Part One

Clearing the
ground

*The forces that distort our relationship
with exercise and self*

CHAPTER 1

It's not that simple, it's not your fault

I'm sure you've already tried to become someone who exercises. You made a plan, bought the gear, and scheduled it in your calendar. Maybe got a few days or weeks in, and then something got in the way. You lost motivation, and the internal story began again. You felt guilty or ashamed, and you told yourself: "If I could just get motivated," or "If I were more disciplined," or "If I could find the right plan, I could finally stick with it," or worse, "Ugh, I'll never get it together, I just can't do it."

This is a story so many people have absorbed about exercise: it's something you do if you have enough willpower and self-control. It's a matter of character, of discipline, of doing it right. And if you're not doing it, there must be something wrong with you.

But this story isn't true. At the very least, it isn't complete.

What if it's not about willpower? What if your resistance to exercise has some wisdom in it? What if you're rejecting a system that makes you feel worse about yourself and almost always fails?

Through all my years working with clients, I've come to realise that it's really not about willpower. Most often, I meet people who are in a complicated, often painful relationship with exercise, a relationship shaped by misinformation, body shame, past injury, rigid rules, guilt, comparison, and a long history of starting and stopping. People who are trying hard, but inside a system that keeps setting them up to fail.

What if it's not about the perfect program, but about the relationship you have with exercise and your body?

REFRAMING THE "PROBLEM"

We know exercise is "good for us." That part's well established. And yet, knowing that hasn't magically made it easier to do. The endless messaging about how great exercise is and how "simple" it should be to start hasn't led to long-term change for most people. If anything, it's created more shame. When someone's been struggling to make movement a habit, hearing again and again how good it is can feel like being told *you should be able to do this by now.* The message lands as: if you're not doing it, something must be wrong with *you.*

And shame is one of the fastest ways to shut down motivation, self-efficacy and self-worth. Sure, it might fuel a short burst of effort, a few "I'll show them!" workouts, but over time, it erodes the very trust and confidence we need to keep going.

The truth is, our relationships with exercise are more complex than willpower or discipline alone can address. If you've struggled to stick with it, you're not alone, *and it's not your fault.*

In fact, the way exercise has been sold to us has often made it harder to build something meaningful. The standard fitness culture messaging has worked its way into how we think about movement, how we think about our bodies, and how we measure progress. Throughout this book, we'll look at those layers with curiosity and compassion and see if we can't make space for something new. But let's start with a story.

A DIFFERENT KIND OF QUESTION

When I first started as a personal trainer, I did what we were taught: ask clients their goals, then set SMART (Specific, Measurable, Achievable, Relevant, Time-bound) objectives to match. Unsurprisingly, one of the most common goals was weight loss, which, interestingly is not what you learn to program for – we learn about cardio, strength, and flexibility. But generally speaking, a program is put together based on these 'surface-level' goals. I started to notice that this approach wasn't really getting to the depth of what people were hoping for, nor the more complex inner struggles they had around exercise.

Some years into training, I started shifting the conversations I was having. Instead of asking the outcomes people were aiming for, I began asking people to tell me about their *relationship* with exercise. What had it been like over the years? What experiences shaped it?

And the stories poured out. People shared their childhood memories of being on sports teams or of being picked last in gym class. They talked about classes they loved, workout kicks they started and stopped, struggles with body image, cycles of dieting, fears of doing it wrong and hurting themselves, and the loop of trying to "be good" only to fall off again.

Suddenly, we weren't just talking about weight loss or strength gains. We were talking about identity, belonging, fears and hopes. There was so much more beneath the surface.

Then I'd ask: *What would you like your relationship with exercise to look like a year from now?*

The answers were very different. I heard things like, "I want exercise to be something I just do, not something I dread," "I want it to feel like a habit that I don't have to motivate myself to do," "I want to feel energetic and do sports again," "I don't want to keep stopping and starting," and "I want my life to feel active and full and to not be afraid."

It became clear that my role wasn't just about building strength or endurance. It was about helping people build a relationship with movement that actually fit their lives, one that felt good, sustainable, and supportive of their wellbeing.

That's the goal of this book: To help you create a relationship with exercise that is life-long, positive, energy-giving, and sustainable.

WHAT THAT TAKES

To get there, we have to do things differently. If we want the relationship to be *sustainable*, we can't keep chasing 30-day challenges or training in ways that leave us depleted and out of balance with the other areas of our lives. If we want it to be *positive*, we can't rely on shame or guilt as motivators. If we want it to be *wellbeing–promoting*, we have to untangle movement from appearance-based goals, because tying exercise for aesthetics can actually undermine its mental health benefits (more on that to come!). If we want it to be *life-long*, we need an approach that can evolve with us through all the seasons of life.

Throughout this journey, we'll unpack the beliefs and baggage we've inherited about exercise, and explore where asking different questions might lead us.

WHAT GETS IN THE WAY

If our goal shifts to building a relationship with exercise that is life-long, positive, energy-giving, and sustainable, then the next natural question is: what gets in the way?

There are a number of barriers to exercise. Some or all may apply to you. Let's go through a few of the most common as it helps to notice what dynamics are at play.

1. Knowledge Gaps AND Information Overload

To get going with exercise, there is a knowledge component. You need a basic level of movement competence. You need to know how to do foundational exercises safely, how to progress gradually, and how to avoid injury. But here's the kicker: the world of fitness information is a weird mix of major gaps and total information overload.

If you search online, you'll find thousands of workout plans and social media instructors offering their spin. But to stand out in a crowded market, most are focused on novelty over fundamentals. The result? Over-complicated routines and a sense that you must be missing something.

The truth is, fitness fundamentals are simple. Maybe even boring. But they work. I once taught a low-impact strength class for women three times a week for years. The workouts were similar every time. People got stronger. More capable. More confident. Because the basics are basic for a reason.

Squats, deadlifts (or just learning how to pick something up well), pressing, pulling, core stability, balance work, these are the building blocks. For cardio? Use your heart rate zones and a progressive plan. That's it. No magic. No gimmicks.

If you don't know how to do the basics, that's a *very manageable* gap. It's a solvable problem that can be addressed to help you feel more confident and like you have a solid foundation.

2. Diet Culture and The Exercise/Weight Trap

This one shows up all the time. I'll ask someone about their relationship with exercise, and I'll get a history of every diet and fitness craze they've ever tried. Keto, paleo, Whole30, intermittent fasting, bootcamps, transformation challenges, etc., the list goes on. (This was the first pattern I noticed when I asked about exercise, that the first response would be about diet!)

We've been conditioned to tie exercise directly to weight loss and body manipulation. But here's the thing: exercise does not cause weight loss. That's not even a controversial opinion, it's what the research tells us, again and again.

Still, diet culture runs deep. It tells us that our bodies must be managed. That our worth is tied to our size. That if we're not actively pursuing thinness through diet and exercise, we're failing.

This creates a toxic feedback loop. Many people start exercising at the same time they start eating less, thinking they're making healthy changes. But the first thing that happens in a calorie deficit? You lose energy. You lose motivation. Your body says, "We're under-resourced. Let's pull back."

This isn't a moral failing. It's your body doing exactly what it's designed to do. If this has been your story, it's SO helpful to know this and start to change this dynamic right away.

If we can begin to unhook the connections between exercise and the roots of diet culture, we can start to experience it differently as something that gives back, not something we do to earn or atone for food.

3. Mindsets and Limiting Beliefs about Exercise

Let's try something. Consider these prompts:

- How long should you work out?
- How hard should it feel?
- How many days a week is enough?
- Is a walk with a friend really "exercise"?
- What happens if you miss a day?

Notice what pops up. Not because there's a right answer, but because most of us carry invisible rules about exercise. Rules we never chose and that often make it harder to engage in movement consistently.

Some of these beliefs come from diet culture. Others come from gym culture, or from exercise science that's aimed at athletes, not everyday people.

We've absorbed the idea that more is always better. That if you're not pushing to your limit, it doesn't count. That "real" workouts must hurt. But here's the thing: that's not how sustainable, life-giving movement works, and it may be undermining both the wellbeing benefits of exercise and your connection to your body.

Professional athletes train at high volumes because their job is performance. They train to peak, and then they rest. Crucially, people are not professional athletes for their whole lives. Bodybuilders train for maximising a specific aesthetic, it's not about health. Neither model is built for the long term. Unfortunately, a lot of fitness culture is built from foundations in both these areas and is due for a rehauling that orients us towards wellbeing and sustainability.

The truth is, most of us don't need "maximum recoverable volume." We need a "minimum effective dosage" that fits our lives and feels good in our bodies, that doesn't leave us soul-crushed and burnt out in the rest of our lives.

4. Interruptions

In the world of 30-day challenges and hard resets, interruption is failure. But in real life, interruption is normal.

You get sick. Your kid gets sick. Work gets busy. You go on vacation. Something throws off your rhythm. The problem isn't that these things happen. The problem is that we think they shouldn't. We treat consistency as never missing a day, when real consistency is the ability to return. To pick up where you are. To adapt.

If your relationship with exercise is flexible and forgiving, it can bend and rebound. If it relies on never being disrupted, every break feels like the end.

5. Time, Money, and Access

Yes, we all have 24 hours in a day. But no, we do not all have the same 24 hours. Some people are parenting small children. Some are working multiple jobs. Some are navigating health challenges or disabilities. Some have limited access to safe exercise spaces, equipment, or supportive communities. If you literally don't have time or capacity, then guilt serves no purpose. Let it go.

But often, what we're really up against is a narrow idea of what counts. We think if we can't do the full hour at the gym, it's not worth it. If we can't afford a membership, we might as well do nothing.

But ten minutes of movement, done with care, can change your day. A walk, some light stretching, a few bodyweight movements, it all counts. The goal is not to do what's ideal. The goal is to do what's possible and meaningful now.

6. Seasons of Life

Your relationship with exercise will change. It should. Parenthood, aging, menopause, injury, illness, career changes, grief - each life season brings shifts in what your body needs and what you can offer it. That's not actually failure, that's your evolution.

What worked for you five years ago may not be suitable now. What you loved in your 20s might not feel good today. That's not a problem to fix. It's a relationship that needs to be updated.

7. Ego Threat

Sometimes, what holds us back is the fear of what it means if we try our best and still fall short. Or a fear of how far we feel from where we once were. Or fear of being a beginner. Again. If you've ever thought, "Why bother? I'll never get back to where I was," you're not alone. But what if the goal isn't to get back? What if the goal is to be in a relationship with your body as it is today?

If you're experiencing any of these barriers, or have in the past, take note of them, and let's see how they might shift and change throughout this journey.

OUR NEW QUESTION

So, what kind of relationship do *you* want with exercise?

Beyond, 'How do I get motivated?' or 'What plan should I follow?' What do you want it to *feel like?* Or bring to your life?

Perhaps you want it to feel like more energy, more strength, as if you have a chance to get grounded, embodied, and connected.

Just like any important relationship, it requires care, communication, boundaries, presence, forgiveness, and trust.

WHERE WE'RE GOING

This book won't give you a perfect plan. But it will help you create something better: a relationship with movement that is yours. That feels good to come home to. That evolves with your life, rather than fighting against it.

We'll explore how to rebuild trust with your body, reconnect with your own signals, and practice movement in ways that are flexible, attuned, and sustaining.

Reflection Point

What would you like your relationship with exercise to be like?

What has made it hard to stay consistent in the past?

What barriers are you currently up against?

CHAPTER 2

Exercise ≠ weight loss, and other hard truths

Many of us came to exercise hoping to change how our bodies look. That desire didn't come out of nowhere. It was modeled, praised, and sold to us as self-improvement and even as self-care. In the short term, it might have felt like motivation, but over time, it likely became something more like pressure, dissatisfaction, or even shame, feeding into a cycle of not-enoughness. It's a great starting point to know that this is *learned*; you weren't born with these beliefs. In fact, as a baby and young child, movement is just who you are. You explore the world, play, run and express without all this baggage. As you grow up, though, you see these cultural messages about bodies, about control of them, and about where exercise fits into all of that.

This chapter isn't about blaming anyone for that. It's about beginning to name and question the beliefs that shaped how we think about movement and exercise in the first place. What if the very goals we were taught to pursue, namely being smaller, leaner, tighter, are part of what keeps our relationship to movement fraught and fragile?

We're going to talk about some of the deeper cultural forces that shape our beliefs about exercise. This can help us gain some clarity to understand the stories we've been handed, and decide if we'd like to choose a different one.

DIET CULTURE AND ITS LEGACY

Diet culture isn't just about 'being on a diet', it's much bigger than that. It's a pervasive system of beliefs that idealizes thinness, equates weight loss with health and virtue, and promotes control over the body as a moral imperative (see Anti-Diet by Christy Harrison for more details). It teaches us that our bodies are problems to be solved, and that the solution is usually discipline, deprivation, and shrinking.

Most of us absorbed this worldview without ever being explicitly taught it. We saw it in magazine covers, family comments, gym posters, social media feeds and even during medical appointments. Thinness was coded as success, and exercise was a tool to get there.

This way of thinking turns movement into a means to an end. It encourages us to disconnect from our bodies in the moment and focus on an imagined future. It flattens exercise into something transactional: how many calories did I burn? What did I earn? Did I do enough? It's hard to connect with your body when you're constantly trying to change it. And also, it literally doesn't work that way. Not only is this harmful to the relationship you have with your body, it doesn't actually lead to the weight control it promises. This in itself isn't 'bad' because larger bodies are just as wonderful as smaller ones, but it is bad that its central promise is based on a lie.

It also doesn't work to just 'separate' exercise from dieting behaviours in other areas because all the domains through which you exist as a body are interconnected, which makes it important and optimal to root out diet culture from your life entirely. Part of my motivation for this book was that a lot of the anti-diet culture and body positive books I was reading, which focused on intuitive eating and leaving diet culture, had only minimal input on exercise, generally focusing on stopping or reducing structured exercise. As we are exploring in this book, there's the potential for a much more nuanced conversation about exercise that doesn't throw the baby out with the proverbial bathwater. For some people, namely those with eating disorders or whose relationship with exercise is very dysfunctional, an entire break with exercise, especially highly structured exercise, for a time might be beneficial; however, it's not only possible to have a relationship with exercise that doesn't enforce diet culture but to have one that help build a positive, attuned connection with the body.

OBJECTIFICATION AND GAZE

Objectification theory helps us understand the psychological consequence of living in a culture that constantly evaluates bodies: we begin to internalize that external gaze. This means we start to see ourselves not from the inside out, but from the outside in. We can imagine a subjective experience of the body when we picture someone moving *unself-consciously.* This is the flip side to objectification.

Through our upbringing, we become aware of how we are perceived by others. Then, instead of noticing how we feel in our bodies, we become preoccupied with how we look. We scan, critique, and manage our appearance as if we're always on camera. We become an object of others' *gaze,* which can become internalized whether others are there or not. Psychology research calls this self-objectification, and it's been linked to increased body shame, anxiety, and reduced ability to experience bodily sensations.

When it comes to exercise, this internalized gaze often means we're turning our bodies into objects to be acted upon rather than connecting *with* them as ourselves. Movement becomes something we do to sculpt, fix, or maintain ourselves and not something we do to feel, explore, or express. This is so common that it's referred to as *normative discontent* that in our society, it's considered normal for women to dislike their bodies, to see them as deficient in their natural state and in continual need of correction and control. This shift erodes our sense of embodiment.

DISCONNECTION FROM EMBODIMENT

Embodiment is the experience of being in and with your body, sensing, feeling, and moving from within. It's what allows us to respond to our needs, notice our emotions, and experience presence. But when we relate to our bodies as projects or objects, that sense of internal connection starts to fade.

Many people who feel "unmotivated" or "lazy" about exercise are actually coping with this disconnection. It's not that they don't care; it's that the version of movement available to them feels more like self-objectification or punishment than self-support. There is actually wisdom in this flavour of resistance. When exercise paradigms encourage dissociation from the body, acting on it like an object for others' enjoyment, and ignoring bodily cues for rest or signs of discomfort, it's no wonder we experience internal conflict.

We can better understand where we currently are in our journey of embodiment by taking a look at the Developmental Theory of Embodiment developed by Niva Piran and colleagues. This body of work represents over 20 years of research grounded in lived experiences of girls and women throughout the lifespan. What's important is that it's not just what we *think* about our bodies, but how we live in them, and embody or reject the values of a society. This experience is shaped by the culture and social environment around us, and also by the developmental stage a person is in. Over time, especially through puberty and the massive body and social structure changes of adolescence, girls and women (and others socialized into objectification) are pulled away from embodied freedom and subjective experience to external control and seeing the body as an object. Tragically, but not at all surprisingly, this experience of disconnection from the body (negative embodiment or disembodiment) is currently the norm through the tumultuous teen years; but whether or not we can return to a place of positive embodiment in adulthood depends on a variety of factors which can be helpful to understand, orient towards, and mindfully cultivate.

The Developmental Theory of Embodiment describes five inter-related domains of the body. People who generally feel connected in one domain tend to feel well connected in the others, and vice versa: when we struggle in one area, it also affects the other domains of embodiment. What is important to understand is that we are not labelling each domain as positive or negative per se, but on a continuum between *freedom* and *control*.

Let's look at each of the domains of embodied experiences one at a time. These domains represent themes and central tensions we navigate throughout our lifespan.

1. Body Connection and Comfort

In this domain, the central question is whether you feel at home in your body or alienated and uncomfortable in your body. What we absorb from society around us is often that we can't trust our bodies and that we must be critical rather than feeling a sense of ease and trust in our bodies.

2. Agency and Functionality

Here, the main dynamic is between experiencing your body as capable and appreciating what it does for you versus something that needs to be fixed or hidden. As this relates to exercise, the disconnection shows up when the purpose of exercise is to shrink and manipulate the body or to 'burn calories' or 'tone up.'

3. Experience and Expression of Desire

This domain describes whether desire is experienced as a normal, embodied experience or as something to suppress, and disconnect from. This domain reflects the relationship a person has with food and eating behaviour. Diet culture and the associated self-objectification make us distrust our hunger and fullness cues and view these as areas in need of control. It also reflects self- vs other-defined sexuality. Gaze encourages us to view the body as something we should try to make sexy for others, and that our sexuality is predominately for other people rather than for ourselves. Both of these dimensions can interrupt the relationship with exercise.

4. Attuned Self-Care

In this domain, whether we care for the body from a place of respect and listening is contrasted with rigid plan following or tracking and the ignoring of needs. With regards to exercise, many focus on obedience and control rather than attunement, which is where exercise has the potential to be real self-care.

5. Resistance to Objectification

In this domain, as introduced above, being in your body subjectively is contrasted with seeing the body from the outside as an object to monitor and display. The challenges in this domain have only been made more difficult as fitness spaces become more performative and less of the private spaces they once were. When we're in the mode of looking at ourselves constantly, it is hard to *be* ourselves fully. Exercise has the potential to be a really potent experience of being in the body, which requires cultivating a resistant stance to objectification and self-objectification.

Now that we've looked at each of the domains briefly, I want to circle back to the central question of *the nature* of each of the embodiment components. Namely, is the relationship one of *freedom or of control*? Across all dimensions, this is the core tension: a feeling of inhabiting the body versus controlling and monitoring the body. Control shows up in our relationship with exercise through the rules, expectations and the focus on the body as an object. Thankfully, freedom, when valued, can be cultivated over time, especially when we can name, understand and metabolize these dynamics in our own lives. Freedom is about self-trust, connection, and presence. All of which can be explored within a movement practice, not just through intellectual understanding.

EMBODIMENT IS RELATIONAL AND POLITICAL

Our embodied realities don't happen in a vacuum. We are the product of all the ecological systems around us: our relationships, culture, the amount of access we have, and the larger systemic forces. What's helpful to know is that these discon-nections are so much more than individual struggles. You are not alone. These patterns of embodied disconnection reflect broader structures, including patriarchy, ableism, racism, capitalism, heteronormativity, and more. The goal is never to dismiss the very real effects of these systems upon us, but to reclaim enough agency and connection to begin to live more fully in our own bodies. Yes, these systems need to change, AND you deserve not to wait any longer to start cultivating something better.

WHEN IT COMES TO EXERCISE

Diet culture and objectification don't just shape how we see our bodies; they shape how we define "real" exercise. Over time, these pressures harden into a set of unconscious rules:

- If it doesn't make you sweat, it doesn't count.
- If it's not intense, it's not effective.
- Rest is weakness.
- More is always better.
- You have to earn your food.
- Exercise is punishment for being "bad."

These beliefs aren't just unhelpful, they're actively harmful. They disconnect us from the feedback our bodies are trying to give and disrupt our embodied experience. They create guilt around rest, anxiety around inconsistency, and shame around doing anything less than "perfect," keeping us stuck in all-or-nothing cycles.

When exercise is framed only in terms of outcomes like weight loss, visible results, and specific numbers, it teaches us to override our body's signals rather than attune to them. We push through pain. We ignore fatigue. We miss the signals our body is sending, and then blame ourselves when we burn out or rebel. This disconnection from the body is one of the biggest reasons people struggle with exercise. The inner conflicts that arise from the version of exercise we're presented with leave us overwhelmed and exhausted before we even begin. When your body feels like a problem and a project, it's hard to sustainably have a good relationship with it. Exercise and movement can become meaningful again when they reconnect us to agency, functionality, and self-trust.

REORIENTING TOWARDS WELLBEING

What if we redefined the point of movement, not as control, not as achievement, but as *care*? As something we do not manipulate the body, but to be in a grounded and attuned connection to it?

Wellbeing isn't only a product of the physical effects of exercise; it can also be something we cultivate through embodied connection. The relationship we build with our bodies through movement can be one of the most powerful ways to shift from judgment to trust, from control to attunement in our exercise relationship and beyond.

When we let go of the need to prove, punish, or fix, we make space for something else: presence, curiosity, freedom, even joy.

If all of this feels personal or challenging, that's really okay. These aren't just ideas, they're stories that have shaped how we live in our bodies. You're allowed to feel grief, anger, or disorientation as you begin to name them.

You're also allowed to start again, not by trying harder, but by listening differently. By remembering that your body is not a problem to solve, and that exercise is not a debt to be paid for your existence. It's a way of relating and a way of reclaiming. We're not 'giving up' on goals; rather, we're expanding your definition of what matters and what's possible. What if the most important result of moving your body wasn't how it changed, but how it let you *come home* to yourself?

CHAPTER 3

The control trap: why we can't out-hustle our bodies

Speaking of uncomfortable truths, we need to talk about control and where it fits into some of our beliefs about exercise that relate to appearance, health, or other hoped-for outcomes. There's a general belief that if we just try hard enough, we can make our bodies look or perform a certain way. We've been exploring the empty promises of Diet Culture, but there's more to unpack here if we're looking for real freedom. The tension we have to navigate is that your body is not an inert object, but it's also not entirely out of our hands. Oftentimes people simply shift from being obsessed with weight and appearance to being obsessed with strength goals, or with health and longevity. These shifts are meaningful and can be a way better place to be, but there may still be a disconnect from a relational, responsive self-connection.

The narratives around control come from a variety of places, including Cartesian dualism (seeing the mind and body as separate and distinct), Puritanical religious messaging about transcending the body and forgoing pleasure, and racist, classist, sexist valuing of certain body types as reflective of moralism and character. These have seeped into the wellness industry's obsession with discipline, willpower, and "transformation." This moralizing is seen most obviously in language choices around "clean eating," "guilty pleasures," "cheat days," "I've been really good lately," etc.

This control trap often wears the mask of self-improvement but is really perfectionism in disguise. Unfortunately, exercise and nutrition are domains where perfectionism is socially rewarded, up to and including behaviours that are risky and disordered. Eating disorders and subclinical disordered eating are frighteningly common, with high mortality risk, high rates of relapse, and life-long health complications even if treated. Compulsive exercise is frequently a part of that dynamic. Even for folks who do not have disordered eating, there can be a lot of anxiety over doing everything "right" and fear about what happens if you don't.

There is a lot of fear-mongering about exercise. For example, if you don't do 150 minutes of cardio per week your heart attack risk is way higher, that if you don't strength train, you'll break a hip and have dementia when you're 80, etc. Like guilt, fear can motivate in the short term, but it's not an effective long-term source of motivation. In fact, fear and guilt often do a fun little pas de deux, creating a cycle that makes you feel worse and worse. Things that make you feel bad will never reliably get you to a place that feels good.

The uncomfortable truth is that neither fitness nor health are the meritocracy they purport to be. Fit bodies are seen to be 'proof' of discipline, morality, and worth, which feeds a misleading idea that effort always leads to a predictable outcome. The truth is that "fit" doesn't have a look, and neither does "health." There's a lot of privilege in this 'earned not given' narrative because people see the hard work they've done and not the barriers they didn't face. You can tell basically nothing about how fit a person is by looking at them, and 100 people doing the same workout program will all end up looking different. Some invisible privileges in fitness include: genetics and predispositions; access to quality food and movement spaces; positive movement role models early in life; safety, time and energy to prioritize health and fitness; and able-bodiedness and neurotypicality. What we aren't talking about when we see fitness and health as purely meritocracy are social determinants of health, including access, education, and physical safety, and the limits of our own control when it comes to health.

There's a tricky balance to be had. Can we somehow both take empowered control over our health AND also accept what the limitations of that control are (and ideally care about the systemic changes that matter)? The limitations of control are part of the human condition and something we would all prefer not to think about. It's great that we're talking about aging well, health-span, and all the empowering things we can do for ourselves, *but* we must stop short of both anxious obsession and self-blame if things don't go to plan. These fears, whether it's about muscle building or cardio capacity, can disconnect us from body signals in favour of rigid planning or expectation, which further erodes trust and connection to the body, leading to the shame cycle, and even burnout.

CONTROL ≠ CARE

There is a fundamental difference between controlling your body and caring for it. An action may be the same, like going to a workout class, but the experience will be different. One of the most interesting pieces of research on embodiment is measuring affect (in-the-moment feelings) of people in a yoga class. In one class the cues are about toning, tightening, and shaping the body's appearance; in another the cues were purely directive (e.g. Place your right hand next to your left foot), in the third, the cues included tuning into the body, (e.g. feeling your body on the mat, and noticing different areas of the body). What was found was that the least mood-boosting condition was the appearance-focused cues, practical cues were in the middle, and the biggest mood-boost was when the cues were about tuning into the body sensations. This matters because it's not just 'oh it's nice to be kinder to yourself.' In a very real way, it impacts the wellbeing benefits of any individual bout of exercise. What if we can create those conditions for ourselves and create a practice of those inner cues to feel the body and notice the sensations? Compared with controlling the body with perfectionism and outside ideals, care is responsive and attuned and can shift any movement experience into a wellbeing boosting practice of self-connection.

WHY "EXERCISE" AND NOT "MOVEMENT" OR SOMETHING ELSE?

In spaces that center attunement, embodiment, and healing, there's often a rebranding of "exercise" as "movement," "joyful movement," or "intuitive movement" as a way of loosening the grip of performative fitness culture and diet culture. Those terms can be great if they resonate with you; use them if you prefer, you get to call it whatever feels most supportive.

I do like to challenge this a little bit, and make space for the word 'exercise' too and that an attuned relationship with movement could even include treadmills, barbells, and varying degrees of structure. Exercise itself was never the problem. The problem is the paradigm we've absorbed around it, the one that tells us our bodies are objects to be shaped, controlled, and perfected and connects our worth to visible outcomes and suggests those who haven't "achieved it" simply haven't tried hard enough. We know this paradigm of control masquerades as care and disconnects us from our bodies, from each other, and from the deeper needs we're trying to meet. And yet, we can still value exercise. We can appreciate how it feels to be strong, how movement can support our mental health, cardiovascular function, or energy levels. We may want to choose some structured forms of training, not because we need to fix ourselves, but because we want to feel more connected, more alive.

This is where our relationship to exercise diverges from healing a relationship with food. With food, we tend to accept that the process will be messy and nonlinear, and we don't expect ourselves to have fully healed from diet culture before we eat lunch. But with exercise, it's different. Many people feel like they can't re-engage until they've resolved all their ambivalence, shed all self-objectifying thoughts, or figured out the "right" way to move again.

But that's not how change works. You don't have to be free of all old patterns before you begin again. Thoughts *will* crop up, and old narratives might whisper. That's not failure, it's the most obvious result of the long-term messaging around you. You're not working toward a perfectly conflict-free connection with exercise. You're building a relationship with your body, one that can hold nuance, complexity, and care.

Exercise can live anywhere along the spectrum from structured to spontaneous. It can be intuitive, expressive and goal-oriented. What matters is the nature of your relationship with it. Are you moving from control or from care?

Questions for Reflection

What does care actually look like or feel like for your body right now?

How would your relationship with movement shift if control wasn't the goal?

CHAPTER 4

You're not lazy - you're tired, scared, and smart

What if part of your resistance is actually wisdom? And that rather than 'laziness,' there's protection? So many of us carry messages like "I always quit," "I'll never get it together," "I'm so lazy," or "I just don't want it enough." Within our resistance to exercise as it's typically presented, this can be an important signal, and not a flaw. Maybe some of it is a resistance to being objectified, to being underfed, over-stressed, or being told what to do. Maybe you're rebelling against systems that have hurt you.

IT'S NOT VANITY, IT'S SAFETY AND BELONGING

It's easy to dismiss the body improvement project as vanity, self-absorption, or superficiality. But for most people, especially women and marginalized folks, the pursuit of a "better" body isn't about ego, it's about safety and survival. We live in a culture where the perfectionism that shows up in work or relationships also lives in our bodies as **embodied perfectionism**. It's the belief that our worth is conditional, and that our bodies are always in need of correction, maintenance, and control. We're taught from a young age that if we can just look right, we'll be accepted, respected, even loved. And because that promise is everywhere, including media, healthcare, dating, and job opportunities, it makes sense that we internalize it.

This in turn affects your nervous system, and *hypervigilance* can become a natural response. When your body and appearance feel closely tied to your social safety, whether it's about being accepted, admired, or simply not judged, you might scan your reflection, feel preoccupied with food or exercise, or get overly stressed when your routine is disrupted. These aren't bad habits; they're protective strategies. Your nervous system is trying to secure belonging.

For many of us, the pressure to conform to body ideals lives in the **fight** response, striving, controlling, grinding toward an unattainable goal. For others, it lives in **freeze**, shutting down, feeling numb or detached, unable to engage with movement because it feels too vulnerable, too overwhelming, or too far from the imagined ideal.

And that's the kicker: the cultural ideal isn't just unattainable; it's *always* shifting, AND our bodies are always changing. Even if we *do* achieve a look that gets praised, we feel the pressure to maintain it. We know, deep down, what it took to get there, and what it would cost to stay there. We feel like frauds even in our "success," because our nervous system never really settles. Because none of this ever truly gives us what we're after: connection, ease, belonging, freedom.

So no, it's not vanity, it's a socially and culturally conditioned and nervous system-mediated attempt to feel safe in a culture that makes us feel like our worth depends on how we look. This is all layered in with our own personal experiences of body shaming, previous attempts that have eroded self-efficacy, and any traumas we may carry, particularly those related to the body.

The truth is that, even if we've bought the promise that changing our bodies will lead to acceptance, love, and self-worth, the truth is: it doesn't work. Exercise (and intentional weight loss by other means), despite decades of marketing, does *not* reliably lead to weight loss. Large-scale, well-established research shows that most weight loss efforts are not sustainable over time, and that shame-based motivation leads to burnout, not resilience.

When we motivate ourselves through criticism and treat movement like penance, we're pouring stress into a nervous system that's already dysregulated. It's like putting sugar in a gas tank and expecting the car to run. This is the most likely outcome of the systems we live within, so we need to be compassionate when we have found ourselves in this place and know that at the root of this cycle is not a failure of willpower, and it can begin to shift when we begin to invite in self-compassion.

Self-compassion is not indulgence or letting ourselves off the hook. It's regulation. It's how we begin to shift from a survival-based relationship with our bodies into one that is grounded, responsive, and real. We can start by naming with kindness that, of course, we've internalized these messages. How could we not? We've all lived inside this system. But we don't have to stay there. And maybe, some of that resistance we've felt has been your body wisely avoiding what has felt unsafe, painful, and shaming.

We can look outward at the people we love - our friends, our partners, our children - and recognize that their worth is not tied to their body size or workout routines. We love them as they are, in all their fluctuations. What would it be like to offer even a sliver of that same grace to ourselves?

When we center compassion, we begin to break the cycle. We stop asking exercise to prove our worth. We begin to imagine what movement could look like if it was no longer about fixing something broken, but about tending to something precious, because if we're not trying to earn our value, maybe we can stop striving and start attuning and move our bodies not to become someone better, but to feel more fully ourselves.

THE CULTURAL LIE OF LAZINESS

Our current over-glorification of 16-step morning routines, 'biohacking', the hyping of overwork and extreme performative productivity has made so many people feel like they are a failure. "Laziness" (which I put in quotes because I don't think it's a real thing) is a moral judgment that gets placed on people who are unsupported, disconnected, burnt out and chronically dysregulated. We're not only disconnected from our bodies for the reasons we've explored so far, but we're also physically and emotionally depleted from emotional labour, stress, unprocessed trauma, and chronic pressure. We need to call this what it is and let out some collective exhales. Beliefs about laziness and guilt are best buddies that sap our motivation and then shame us. When it comes to exercise, maybe many of us need restorative and regulating movement practices before 'building' anything, and that's not only okay, but likely ideal. If your life in general is very depleting, your movement should balance it out rather than make things worse. If your life is in a period of relative smoothness, and you enjoy it, maybe there's room for more intensity, etc. But if you're mentally and emotionally trashed, trashing your body on top of it is not a great idea, which is what dominant fitness paradigms suggest we do.

FEAR

Many people experience fear as a component of their relationship to exercise. There are a lot of layers, including fear of pain, fear of failure, of visibility, of comparison to others or a past version of yourself, or of what it means if you try again and still struggle. Avoidance in these cases; where there is known pain, physical or emotional; makes sense. Your nervous system has likely learned to associate exercise with threat. That's not laziness or self-sabotage; it's protection. Later in the book, we'll explore fear in more depth, how it lives in the body, how it shapes our patterns, and how, if exercise is something you want to do, you can build more safety and comfort into how you approach exercise.

WHAT IF EXERCISE DIDN'T HAVE TO PROVE ANYTHING?

Now that we've explored removing the carrot of appearance and hustling for worthiness, what's left? We can envision our movement and exercise practices as a physical alignment with our values, a practice of attuning to our bodies and noticing what feels good and has value for us, separate from what has been modelled, an opportunity to build trust, a space to practice listening, and ultimately a way to live more authentically in our bodies and not perform our existence. This relationship with movement is one that shifts over time, and we've begun by clearing the ground of some of the disrupting forces, and now we are beginning to envision what a new way of relating could offer.

Part Two

Reimagining the relationship

Building a new internal compass, rooted in self-compassion and embodiment

CHAPTER 5

Starting from self compassion

We've just unpacked a lot of the tangled web that's been surrounding our relationship with exercise, and after all of that, you may be wondering, *what now?* After naming the forces that have shaped our experience, like shame and control and cultural ideals, we now have a chance to begin again, this time grounded in self-compassion, motivation that arises from within, and a more profound sense of embodiment. This journey of disillusionment with some of the systems around us and the ways in which we've engaged in them is not always easy and not always linear. It doesn't have to all be figured out at once. While still being deeply reflective, we will start to explore things with some practicality, as well as create space for you to begin your own embodied exploration. As we've already begun exploring, the central shift in how we relate to movement and exercise is from one of shame and control to one of self-compassion and attunement. We'll continue to challenge the rhetoric that harshness and judgment drive changes and begin practicing a more sustainable source of energy in the form of self-kindness as we unlearn body perfectionism.

WHY SELF-COMPASSION COMES FIRST AND HOW TO BEGIN

We are often so much harsher to ourselves than we would ever be with others. When we're coming from a place of harshness, we're always having to push harder to get moving rather than releasing some of the tethers that have been holding us back. Sustainable change doesn't come from force, but rather from freeing up this relationship. We cannot shame ourselves into self-love. All real lasting growth has to have a foundation of self-compassion in order to last.

All well and good, you may be thinking, but how do I practice this? First and foremost, you need to know that these body-critical thoughts, fears, and judgments *are going to happen.* Even when we know all about the science, psychology, and justice sides of it all, the thoughts *are* going to crop up because they've been conditioned. In the shame-based model we've absorbed, the fitness industry has often used its marketing to amplify our discomfort, and it's no wonder we've absorbed it. When these thoughts creep up, many people suggest things along the lines of telling that critical part of us to 'shut up' or to immediately focus away from it and supplant it with some sort of positive reframe. I'm actually going to suggest we do the opposite and deal with these thoughts that come up in a different way. We need to acknowledge the pain this has caused us rather than ignoring and pushing it away. If you have the thought, for example, "Ugh I'm so lazy" when you don't feel like working out, rather than telling that inner critical voice to 'shut up' or to cognitively counter with "no I'm not because XYZ" can we slow down enough to really feel, "ouch" that really hurts to not just be called lazy but to feel that I am lazy? To get curious enough to gently explore where we might have picked that up and really connect and care for the part of you that picked up this belief. We can imagine how we'd support a child or a dear friend who came to us and shared this painful moment of self-judgement, or if you can, connect with that younger version of yourself who absorbed this belief. When we meet the judgmental sides with nurturing, rather than shoving them down, we're meeting ourselves with the softness we deserve. There are more in-depth practices I love to use for working in this type of way, including the RAIN practice (recognise, allow, investigate, nurture) developed by Tara Brach and the Internal Family Systems method of working with parts developed by Richard Schwartz, but we shouldn't under-estimate the healing that can happen in these small moments when we acknowledge, 1) ouch, that judgemental thought is painful; 2) validate that it makes sense that belief is there given the context; and 3) chose to feel caring and nurturing towards that in-pain part of you. Before I even knew about these more formal practices and modalities like IFS and RAIN, I'd been exploring this within myself and my own relationship to exercise, and with clients and theirs in this organic way, by finding an ounce of curiosity and softness, and I have found it to be incredibly impactful.

An oft-used metaphor is that self-compassion is like a muscle and we strengthen it over time, and there is some utility in that, but even more so, I think of it as an orientation to ourselves and the journey we're on for which there's no specific 'destination' we're arriving at. Rather than needing to have a relationship with exercise that has zero tension, never any resistance, and is completely judgement-free, we need one which allows us permission to be human and to be able to work with these things *as they come up.* We are human beings existing as dynamic bodies; it makes sense that we might navigate some challenges, but we become strong sailors by knowing we can weather the storms. In this way, self-compassion fuels our sustainability, our resilience, and provides a safe landing from which to explore something new. Self-compassion can help soften all the areas where we've had resistance, are afraid to fail, and can help build the safety necessary to start exploring a new way of relating. As we begin to meet ourselves with more compassion, something profound shifts in how we understand and relate to our past and present. From this more grounded place, we can begin to recognize a deeper kind of knowing, a greater clarity that comes from aligning our lived experience with our values.

ALIGNED KNOWING

Self-compassion can be misconstrued as 'letting yourself off the hook' but it can actually be what clears enough space for real authentic growth. This is the foundation of moving from control to care. When it comes to our relationship with exercise, there's this moment of "Head, Heart and Gut knowing" that lets us know that we're not going back to the way it used to be. Head-knowing appeals to our logical side, seeing the research that exercise doesn't lead to weight loss and that focusing on appearance undermines wellbeing benefits of exercise. Heart-knowing can connect to our justice-orientation when we consider the real harm done by fatphobic systems impacting access, medical care, and psychological damage. Gut-knowing and connecting these through our own narratives and experiences with dieting, exercise, or unsustainable previous attempts with exercise, we can notice that these never worked, never truly delivered on their promises, and created disruption within us. When we can see all of this and practice holding it with self-compassion, what we create is going to feel completely different.

SMALLEST POSSIBLE EXPERIMENT

If you're curious to start exploring this concept in motion, now might be a good time to start a little experiment where the goal is not exercise itself, but to notice *what comes up* when we exercise and see if we can extend a little bit of self-compassion when it does. If you are already doing some form of physical activity, the practice arena is already set up, and you'll start noticing where thoughts and beliefs pop up; whether it's to push a bit harder, that you need to stay the whole hour, body-checking, etc. If you aren't exercising, pick something tiny (like so tiny it's basically already done) and notice what emerges. Possible choices like walking to the end of the block, stretching for 2 minutes, or dancing to one song can all be meaningful opportunities to notice what comes up. This might seem deceptively small, but that's the point. It starts the iterative process of noticing, softening, and learning and is a way to begin embodying a new relationship with movement, one compassionate micro-moment at a time. We need this self-compassion loop in the process because *knowing is not enough.* When we pause and offer kindness or non-judgment in the smaller moments, we're beginning to explore a new way of being; this, in turn, can foster self-efficacy.

A COUNTER-INTUITIVE PERMISSION SLIP

You have unconditional permission to not exercise. Whether that means never exercise again, take a break, or wherever in between. Not that you need it from me, but giving this permission to yourself is counter-intuitively what you need to set yourself free from a tension and judgment-filled relationship with exercise. When we are "should"ing about exercise, tying it up with moral judgement or personal efficacy we're unintentionally undermining our motivation by tying it all up in shame. Shame is the worst long-term motivator because it labels us as fundamentally a loser and looks for evidence to back that up – you didn't make it to the gym today, looks like you really are a loser after all and last week's workouts were a fluke and we're back to the standard loser baseline. Where that leaves us is feeling like we can't do anything to change this fundamental fact about ourselves and that we shouldn't bother trying or pretending to be anything but someone who can't get it together with exercise.

What we want instead is to know that our worthiness as a human being has nothing to do with whether or how much we exercise or don't exercise. If we want to explore a new way of having movement and exercise in our lives, we need curiosity, which is at the opposite end of the spectrum as judgement. Can I explore a new path forward with exercise? Can I try some things, explore, and have enough spaciousness to see that the popular culture version of fitness is not all there is? Can I open my mind to the idea that exercise could even be something I enjoy, even if I haven't enjoyed it in the past?

EMBODYING A GROWTH MINDSET

Once we've created space through permission and softened the hold of shame, we open the door to something new: a relationship with movement that is not about fixing ourselves, but about discovering what we're capable of. This is where the idea of growth comes in, not just as a concept, but as something we can feel and experience in our bodies. This experience of growth can then become transformational to your greater life, sense of self-efficacy, and mindset orientation towards life. The foundational work on *Mindset* comes from researcher Carol Dweck, who described two fundamental orientations towards ourselves, which not only relate to our beliefs but shape how we interact with the world through approach or avoidance strategies and thus in turn shape the structures of our lives. These are the *fixed mindset* and the *growth mindset.* The fixed mindset is a general perception that your abilities are limited, set in stone, and that challenges are threatening to your sense of self and should be avoided. The growth mindset, alternately, is a perception that success is dictated by effort, we have autonomy to shape our lives, and challenges are opportunities for growth. Unsurprisingly, there are a whole host of benefits associated with a growth mindset, partly because the beliefs we hold shape the choices we make and you can't achieve things if you don't try. Cognitively, we understand this with ease. In practice, many (or most) of us have all kinds of fixed mindsets about ourselves as exercisers, about exercise more generally, and about our relationships with ourselves and with the world. We'll challenge a lot of these beliefs throughout the book, but I want to focus just now on exercise itself as a physical experience of a growth mindset. Exercise offers us a tangible feedback loop: as your strength grows, you can lift something with ease that felt hard last month, your endurance feels different when you go on a hike, or you notice your skills and coordination developing over time through your effort and your natural adaptations. There is a difference in noticing this sort of adaptation, growth and responsiveness that differs from the body manipulation that turns the body into an object. We can think of this as providing conditions for growth versus controlling outcomes. This felt-experience of knowing that you are strong, resilient, capable of growth and change has the potential to spill over to the rest of your life as well by challenging some of these long-held beliefs, like "I'm not athletic" "I'll never get it together" we can see that a lot of these labels and limitations are beliefs and not the capital T truth. There's something that is especially impactful about this experience being *embodied* as opposed to cognitive, which can be especially helpful. This is supportive of overall wellbeing as it bolsters our sense of *self-efficacy,* which is our belief in our own agency and ability to grow and effect change in the world. Attuned exercise experiences give us tangible experience attuning to our bodily cues and sensations, setting and meeting self-chosen goals, and navigating challenges and novel experiences with curiosity rather than fear.

It sounds fairly meta to apply a growth mindset to your relationship with exercise which gives you tangible experiences of growth mindset in action and your overall self-efficacy and orientation to yourself can begin to shift. It *does* work though, specifically because it's via the domain of the body and centres our lived experience. This gives us the chance to learn from physical feedback without shame, practice self-trust, embody agency, and witness our own increasing capacity. These felt-sense experiences of attuning to body needs of when to rest and when you can push, to notice what feels good and enjoyable, to practice showing up for yourself in your life with self-compassion, and to know your own strength and resilience are a gift beyond the shallow promises of the fitness industry as usual. It can be *so much more.*

COUNTERING THE PARADIGM WE'VE ABSORBED

As we've explored, much of the fitness industry thrives on amplifying discomfort with how you are right now and drives sales based on the not-good-enough feelings we might have. This creates a tension, resistance, and burnout cycle where we don't receive what's promised and we blame ourselves. This issue is connected to larger cultural systems and the closer influences around us and is connected to larger themes of embodied perfectionism and normative discontent. These societal standards promise safety and belonging, but it's a no-win system with moving targets that never really deliver. On the science side, we know that solid meta-analysis shows that exercise doesn't reliably lead to weight loss, any intentional weight loss is not maintainable long-term for almost everyone, and that shame and self-criticism aren't just ineffective motivational strategies, they are emotionally draining, dysregulating and harmful. Self-compassion and developing a growth mindset help build more psychological safety within ourselves, which allows for true growth, not just 'change.' Self-compassion helps us move through resistance, unhook from unhelpful messages, regulate your system and allow you to take more agency. We can re-learn what care looks like by extending the love we show others to ourselves. We don't treat the people we care about as problems to be solved, and we can explore showing up to movement without anything to prove.

A NEW VISION

The body fixing project is an attempt to soothe our fears of not belonging and unworthiness, self-compassion offers a path toward real, rooted safety. We have permission to be a learner, to be curious, and to make mistakes as we explore. The relationship with exercise can then become sustainable because it allows your whole self to show up, beyond the setting of goals, with room for imperfection, exploration, and trying again as needed.

CHAPTER 6

Motivation that lasts (or, why kicking your own ass doesn't work)

Generally speaking, most people have heard the terms "intrinsic" and "extrinsic" motivation before; the former being motivation that comes from within, and the latter driven by outside pressures. We also tend to understand that, for most things, "intrinsic motivation" is considered better or more sustainable.

But what often gets missed is that motivation doesn't exist as an either/or. It's a *continuum,* and there are many shades in between. What's also often missing is direction: how to actually shift from one form of motivation to another, or how to cultivate a form that supports the kind of relationship we want with movement.

HERE'S A DIAGRAM OF THAT CONTINUUM:

Non-self-determined behavior			Self-determined behavior	Self-determined behavior

←——————————————————————————————→

	Extrinsic Motivation			Intrinsic Motivation
External regulation	Introjected regulation	Identified regulation	Integrated regulation	Intrinsic regulation
External rewards and punishments	Internal rewards and punishments	Personal importance of an activity	Synthesis with the self	Interest, enjoyment, and satisfaction

Controlled motivation	Autonomous motivation

Self-Determination Theory (based on Ryan & Deci, 2000).

Don't worry if it looks complicated or includes new terms, I'll walk you through a clear example and then relate it to exercise and how to start cultivating a range of supportive motivational sources.

LET'S TALK ABOUT BRUSHING YOUR TEETH.

For most of us, brushing our teeth is a habit that lives somewhere along the spectrum of extrinsic motivation. But hang on, wasn't extrinsic motivation the "bad" one? The one based on fear or pressure? Not necessarily. Let's walk through each category on the continuum using tooth brushing as our example:

- **External regulation** is motivation-driven purely by external rewards or punishments. As a kid, this might've been getting in trouble for not brushing, or fearing cavities, bad breath, or someone saying something about it.
- **Introjected regulation** includes internal rewards and punishments. This could sound like, *"I'm a good person because I brush,"* or *"I'm gross if I don't."* It's still controlled, but now by *internalized* pressure or self-judgment.
- **Identified regulation** is a shift toward autonomy. Here, brushing is something you personally value. You understand its importance, and it matters to you. You're not doing it out of shame or fear, but because it aligns with what you care about.
- **Integrated regulation** is even more autonomous. Brushing your teeth is now entirely woven into your wider sense of self and how you care for your body. It's just one small expression of a bigger commitment to caring for yourself with consistency and respect.

On the far end of the spectrum is **intrinsic motivation**, ie, doing something for the sheer enjoyment of the act itself. So, if you genuinely *love* the feeling or ritual of brushing your teeth because it's so fun (and if that's you, live it up), that would be intrinsic motivation. But for most of us, brushing is not about joy; it's about value and alignment.

This example helps illustrate a key point: **extrinsic and intrinsic motivation are not black-and-white opposites**, and trying to force ourselves into "intrinsic motivation only" mode can set us up to fail, especially for something like exercise.

MOTIVATION AND EXERCISE

When it comes to exercise, intrinsic motivation might look like any kind of movement you enjoy purely for its own sake, like walking in the park, dancing at a wedding, gardening, or playing pickleball (though there are super serious pickleballers, too). These are important spaces to explore. You might even write a list: *What kinds of movement would I do even if they didn't "count" toward fitness or health?*

But again, intrinsic motivation isn't always accessible, nor is it the only positive, aligned version of exercise that exists. Let's walk through the types of **extrinsic motivation** using exercise as an example.

- **External regulation**: Exercising because others are watching, or out of a desire to change your appearance and be perceived differently. It could also be fear of judgment if you *don't* work out.
- **Introjected regulation**: Exercising to avoid feeling like a failure, or to feel like a "good" person. Self-criticism and internalized judgment are the drivers here.
- **Identified regulation**: Now we're moving into more autonomous territory. Maybe you exercise because it

supports your mental health or helps you manage energy and stress. It's important to you for a bigger reason, not just because someone told you it should be.

- **Integrated regulation**: Exercise is now strongly linked to your values, your way of relating to your body, and your broader commitment to wellbeing and self-care.

For most of us, our relationship with exercise is layered, and not only one category. For example, when I was taking lots of dance classes during undergrad, I primarily did it because I genuinely enjoyed dancing. But part of me was also hoping, maybe even assuming, it would lead to some appearance changes as a "bonus." Both were true at once. We can be motivated by personal meaning and aligned values *and* still have thoughts shaped by self-criticism or control. That's normal. What matters is learning to notice what we're working with. If your motivation has mostly been fueled by reward and punishment, especially shame or guilt, that's a high-energy system to maintain. It can "work" for a while, but it tends to break down. Autonomous motivation, on the other hand, *requires far less emotional energy* to sustain. It's more durable because it comes from a deeper place.

CULTIVATING MOTIVATION THAT COMES FROM WITHIN

So, how do we actually begin to foster a relationship with exercise that feels aligned with who we are, something that supports motivation that lasts? From the above definitions, identified and integrated motivation, alongside intrinsic motivation. We can't force intrinsic or integrated motivation. These aren't checklist items we tick off; they grow, gradually, as a result of **how we relate** to movement and to ourselves. This is where motivation intersects with the idea of building a relationship. And that relationship, like any other, thrives when it's built on trust, care, and resonance. As mentioned above, intrinsically motivated exercise is anything you are doing purely for fun, enjoyment, or recreation with no specific outcome. What can help in fostering more connection with this motivational energy is two-fold. Firstly, being more generous in what we 'count' as exercise. Perhaps this is one area where the term 'movement' may fit better for many people. Whether it's catching up with a friend while taking a walk, doing some gardening, or having a dance around the living room, we can include this activity in our understanding of our total movement and appreciate the value of this more. Secondly, we can purposely invite and make room for these activities in our lives and know that they don't require extra motivational energy aside from the intentionality or perhaps a bit of planning. Knowing that these things we love to do have value regardless of how other people may 'count' them as exercise or not. When I think of myself, there is almost nothing I enjoy more than having a walk with a friend (especially in nature) and having a good conversation. It's not a 'workout' in the way fitness culture may define it, but it still contributes to my overall wellbeing and physical activity level.

In this category, I'd also include social dancing, trying new activities like paddleboarding or snowshoeing, and gardening.

We can also choose to count 'incidental' activity in our overall conceptualization of exercise in this spirit of being more generous with our definition. This includes things like tidying the house, the walking portions of a commute, taking the kids to the park, walking to the store for errands, etc. These are things we are doing anyway, but now choosing to include in our definition of exercise or movement, which thus require no additional motivation, but which can be accentuated when we choose, like parking a little further away and other such strategies to include a bit more movement in a low-hanging fruit sort of way.

Integrated and intrinsic motivation emerge more easily when exercise is connected to who we are, rather than what others have told us to be; when it's aligned with our values rather than motivated by fear or guilt; and when it feels like a form of self-caring or self-expression, rather than control or correction. This is where the work of attunement comes in. As we practice listening to our bodies and start being honest about what motivates us, what actually feels good in our body, and what feels nurturing and supportive to our whole selves, we start to rebuild trust. With this greater sense of trust, motivation becomes less about self-manipulation and more about self-alignement.

Consider: During what kinds of activities do you feel the most *yourself*? What are some of your most authentic-feeling values and strengths? How could those values or strengths be reflected in your approach to exercise?

LET GO OF THE FANTASY OF PURE INTRINSIC MOTIVATION

It's also helpful to release the pressure to always feel deeply inspired. Motivation is a moving target, and there will always be days when movement feels exciting or joyful and days when it feels less inspiring. When we make choices in alignment with our care for ourselves, rather than enthusiasm, that's okay once we've done the work of releasing the guilt and pressure. This may be akin to the motivation for going to the dentist; we may not *enjoy* it, but we know it's important to our overall self-care. I often use the analogy of a 'little push' or a 'big push' when it comes to doing some exercise. If it takes a small push to overcome inertia, that's okay. If it's going to require a big push, then that's a day to prioritize rest, or other types of nurturing self-care. We make this easier in other ways by adjusting our expectations and the structure of exercise, which we'll explore in more detail in the following chapter.

The real goal is not to live in a permanent state of "wanting" to move, but to build a relationship with exercise that's stable and kind enough that you *return* to it, even after breaks or resistance. A relationship where you're not constantly in conflict with yourself, and that is aligned with your greater values and self-care intentions. That's the kind of motivation that lasts because it's connected to something more.

CHAPTER 7

This isn't just another habit

There is a lot of discussion about building the habit of exercising, and there are aspects of this that may be valuable, but I believe that exercise is quite different from other habits and that we need to meet that complexity with realism, self-compassion, and nuance. Compared with building other habits like flossing or making your bed, exercise requires an ongoing input of significant energy, it can be a lot more emotionally loaded, and as we've explored, it is very much intertwined with our self-identity, appearance related burdens, and sometimes even trauma. Movement lives at an intersection of embodiment, stories of performance or perfectionism, and intense socio-cultural narratives and therefore for a lot of people it requires a different approach.

"PRODUCTIVITY LOGIC" AND YOUR BODY

In our fast-paced, efficiency-driven world, there is a temptation to approach exercise as another to-do list item to be optimized. This is why 'bio-hacking,' tracking of metrics, outcome goal setting, and the vibe of 'pushing through' show up a lot in the discourse around exercise. However, our bodies are not objects nor machines and when we view them as such, it can backfire when the rigid expectations we fail to live up to lead to burnout and the familiar shame spiral. It would be easy to dismiss as failing at a simple habit, when really you're navigating something living, layered, and rich in meaning.

Movement is different from other habits because, as we've explored in the discussion of the developmental theory of embodiment, our relationship with exercise and the body is connected to complex, multi-faceted layers of meaning. Because of this, exercise can surface deep vulnerabilities about how we see and feel about our bodies. Many exercise spaces feel public, and there is an increase in body self-consciousness to even show up, not to mention our long histories of self-efficacy that may be caught up as well. Fitness culture often ties exercise with self-worth, appearance, and productivity which are the cycles we're trying to break, which makes the notion of 'habit' not so simple. Add to that, as mentioned above, that unlike most other habits, exercise takes much more energy and our energy to get moving is affected by other life stresses, hormones, sleep, and mental health.

MONITORING CAPACITY, RATHER THAN FOCUSING ON WILLPOWER

Your energy and capacity are dynamic; it's not just "how bad you want it," but what you actually have the bandwidth for. Rather than pretending we're robots who should always feel precisely energized, we need to normalize and have compassion for the periods of time when our capacity is lower. When life stresses are high, the added load to your life from exercise should naturally be a bit less, or on days you feel lower, there should be an ability to adjust. We need permission to build from where we are, not what we think we "should" be doing. We need to scaffold ourselves for success rather than setting our sights way too high and feeling like we can't live up. What if strength meant trusting your body to evolve over time, not mastering it like a machine?

SUPPORTIVE STRUCTURE VERSUS EXTERNAL YARDSTICKS

Really, what we're doing here when we're unpacking the disruptions between our body and ourselves, and the things that come between us and a positive relationship with exercise, is unsubscribing from the externally dictated measures of our worthiness to re-centre them back within us as something inalienable from who we are. While we're on that journey, it's tempting to assume the correct amount of structure is zero and to be fully in the moment, intuitively expressing ourselves. And that can be great, and honestly needed for many people for periods of time. I do believe, however, that there can be room for some degree of supportive structure if it's something you're craving. Between the extremes of obsessive tracking and aimless improvisation, there's an entire continuum to be explored to choose what feels right for you in this chapter. You can ask yourself the question, *is this plan supporting me or judging me?* Is it designed to pass/fail, or measure your success, or to provide you with some planning, guidance, and support in a way that adds value without causing harm or self-judgement? As an example, a general plan of three mornings per week of workouts that has a more 'basic' version for when you're short on energy or time, and an 'extended' version for when you want to add more and have the time and energy to do so. Where, if in a given week something comes up, there's flexibility, and it's not the end of the world if a workout is skipped, shortened, or made simpler. It provides *some* structure regarding when and what, but allows for a lot of flexibility. It's also completely normal to have seasons in your life where there is more or less structure depending on what else is going on. Creating a version of structure that both lowers the bar to entry and can be modulated based on energy can ironically help more with consistency over a long period of time than the rigid, high intensity model we often see.

TO TRACK OR NOT TO TRACK: A NUANCED VIEW.

Tech-based tracking has become ubiquitous in the current world, which has aspects that can be both helpful and harmful. When I was looking for a watch I could connect to a heart-rate monitor, I found it was literally impossible to find one that didn't also give me a daily step count, and calculate calories burned in my workouts (both things I've chosen to move away from). For those who have struggled with an eating disorder or subclinical disordered eating, the slippery slope of hyper focusing on all the data around food, steps, and calories can be dangerous. However, I've heard from a number of people that the information from their smart watches has helped validate their physical experience and be more self-compassionate, when, for example, they've generally neglected their sense of fatigue and need for rest and felt guilt about not pushing through but their watch's sleep tracker and 'body battery' shows they are physiologically depleted they have the data to challenge the internal narratives. The goal of course, is to listen to the body and be compassionate to the felt-sense, but for those who've struggled with less self-compassion and discounting of physical sensations, the data can help to connect the two. In my own experience, after a significant period of low/no structure in my exercise life, I was recovering from a concussion and some associated health issues. I chose to follow a heart rate zone-based program as there was evidence that this helps with the specific issues I was having. For a few months I followed the plan, and it did work and tremendously benefited my recovery. Other rehab or physio-type exercises can also be fully values-aligned, while being quite structured. On the flip side, if you begin to feel as if a workout 'didn't count' if you forgot your Garmin; that if you adjusted the prescribed program, then you're a quitter; or if missing a workout affects your self-efficacy, it's time to recalibrate the relationship to structure and tracking. When it comes to all the high-tech wearables, you'll be the one to decide if and when you engage with them. The information can potentially have value; however, if it becomes obsessive to optimize all aspects of your physiology and another form of physical perfectionism and a distraction from the rest of your life and from connecting to your felt connection to your body, you can also choose to opt out.

I'd like to add a short note about food tracking and exercise. While an in-depth discussion is beyond the purview of this book, the pervasiveness of food-tracking in fitness spaces deserves mention. From suggesting protein targets to weighing and logging of all foods, the recommendations can vary by environment or by trainer. While I believe most of this advice is well-intentioned, it's important to know that fitness professionals are not qualified to give this type of recommendation and are woefully ignorant of the risks of disordered eating, with most not even screening at all for eating disorder history. The only potential benefit of gym-centric food tracking can be noticing when an athlete or exerciser has been under-eating. Under-eating is very common amongst women generally, and active women in particular, as 'healthy' eating is associated with less energy-dense foods. This type of periodic check-in can be useful *for some people,* but should be short term, not about weight loss, and a source of neutral information not judgement. Ideally, intuitive eating is an optimal landing place, but which may require some scaffolding for some people. If you are highly active and seeking nutritional advice, consider consulting a qualified dietician or nutritionist (ideally one who is not promoting weight loss) rather than a coach or trainer at your local gym.

SITTING ON THE PARK BENCH OR THE BUS BENCH

Trainer Dan John, one of the world's top strength and athletics coaches, has given me my favourite exercise metaphor that helps re-frame our exercise intentions in a more sustainable way. He shares the idea of 'bus bench' versus 'park bench' workout. When you're sitting on a bus bench, it's *because you want to get somewhere* - you're waiting for the bus to take you where you want to go. When you sit on a park bench, you're just hanging out, looking around because *it's nice to be there.* 'Bus Bench' workouts are ones where you're hoping for a specific result; it's structured and there is an expected outcome in a specific timeframe. 'Park Bench' workouts are to enjoy moving your body, maybe with more variety and less intensity, and just being in the moment. Many people focus on, or believe they should be focusing on, 'bus bench' workouts most or even all of the time. But for the long term, according to Dan John, you should spend the majority of your time on the proverbial park bench. Somewhere around 75% - 80% is his suggestion. Where maybe one workout out of 4 or 5 is focused on really specific things, or once per year doing a program focused on strength or cardio (if you want to). What's remarkable about this re-frame is that this comes from one of the top strength and conditioning coaches in the world, and that this perspective sets us free from feeling like we always have to do some sort of focused program that we're giving our all to. Sure, if strength is a goal, that can be *part* of your exercise life but it doesn't have to be a chasing of strength by gritting your way through it for your entire life. It's ok (and beneficial!) to do some more general, feel-good, moderate intensity workouts most of the time, and maybe once a week do a more focused workout, or once a year focus on a 6-12 week program for increasing strength. How freeing! Most of the time, you can do basically anything and still have great improvements in your fitness without feeling burnt out, needing the gallons of motivation necessary to train hard, and always recovering from the hard training. It reminds me of once when I was taking a powerlifting seminar. It was hosted at a known powerlifting gym, the gym owner was there, and I mentioned in passing that maybe at some point I'd reach out about having him make me a program, and his reply was, "Why? All the best programs are online for free; they're basic, but they work." In the industry of fitness, there are all kinds of folks selling all kinds of programs, but really, it does not have to be super complicated. For most people, workouts that are short, simple and moderately intense are perfect. Far from slacking, this shift is wise and strategic to help your relationship with exercise be sustainable.

PUTTING THIS INTO PRACTICE

In this chapter, we've explored why exercise isn't the same as other habits because of the energy it takes and the complexity of our embodied experiences. We've introduced the idea of supportive structure, explored some of the nuances of tech and tracking, and explained why spending some time on the park bench is a great idea. Let's now walk through some examples of how this could look in practice. For someone who enjoys group classes, this may look like a selection of classes, each with no through-line and letting go of the idea that you need more structure. It might include a couple of days a week ear-marked for "cardio" but the flexibility to choose a hike with a friend, a machine workout, or walking the dog and to adjust the timing based on schedule and energy needs. It could be a basic strength plan with 2-3 main exercises and a general rep range with a goal of slow, steady progress over a long period of time. Perhaps it's a "movement menu" you've created for yourself, offering different, scalable options to choose from. Maybe it's doing those physio exercises and also getting in a few balance/core exercises that feel good on days when there is room.

Key components, for those you like some structure, include having a simple plan with flexibility built in, room for energy fluctuations, and, if it suits you, the possibility of some degree of tracking for *awareness*, rather than accountability or measuring success. You can also consider using a form of tracking to keep note of *how you felt*, or use journaling to continue the ongoing work of self-compassion with external pressure messaging that crops up. You're allowed to do exercise differently than the way it's been presented, and this shift isn't about making exercise easy, but about making it sustainable for the long-haul. In the grand scheme of your whole life, self-compassion, attunement, and supportive structure are more powerful and longer-lasting than any 'willpower hack.' Building this new relationship with exercise that works for your actual life, body, and capacity isn't weakness, it's wisdom.

CHAPTER 8

Joy is a legitimate goal

When people ask me how I stay consistent with exercise, they often assume it's discipline or willpower. But the truth is simpler and kinder: I enjoy it. Joy is what sustains me. Enjoyment of movement is what calls me back.

That might sound surprising if you've spent years wrestling with guilt, pressure, or perfectionism around exercise. But joy is not a reward you earn from "doing it right," it's something you can begin with. It's also why I don't need to summon motivation to move every day; movement has become aligned with my values, my broader definition of self-care, and a chance to continue connecting with my embodied self. That alignment, and the pleasure that comes from it, makes it easy.

Many of us need to reclaim joy, pleasure, and playfulness, not as indulgences, but as deeply valid reasons to move (and ways to be outside of the gym as well). When we've been taught that our bodies are objects to control or projects to perfect, we lose access to the joy and expression movement can offer. But joy is a kind of resistance. It pushes back on dominant cultural narratives of discipline, control, and fear, and invites levity, curiosity, and connection instead. Think of how children naturally dance, climb, run and explore. That was you too. We just became separated from our natural way of being through socialization. Movement, expression and joy really are your birthright.

MOVING TOWARD WHAT FEELS GOOD

I absolutely love how I feel when I'm active, both during movement and in the ripple effects across my days when I've been consistently active. But not everyone starts there. For many of us, the belief that only "hard" things count has undermined the wellbeing benefits of moving our bodies.

The truth is, intense exercise tends to benefit mood for people who are *already athletic,* but for those who are new to movement, it's often a *gentler activity* that brings the biggest boost in mood and wellbeing. When we begin where we feel safe, supported, and well-resourced, we also build trust in our bodies. We start developing interoceptive awareness (the ability to sense our internal state) that we can attune to rather than overriding bodily signals in the name of toughness.

Attuned movement doesn't mean avoiding challenge; it means having the tools to navigate effort with discernment. In this space, comfort, joy, and safety aren't distractions, they're signals worth paying attention to, both for the short term and long-term benefits. Feeling good is a sign you're on the right path, not a sign you're slacking off.

MOVEMENT'S ROLE IN EMOTIONAL REGULATION

While the focus of this book isn't on listing the benefits of exercise, I would be remiss not to speak to one of its most profound effects: emotional regulation.

Movement helps us metabolize stress. In their book *Burnout*, Emily and Amelia Nagoski describe exercise as a way to complete the stress cycle, which helps to restore our emotional equilibrium, not just burn off steam. When we move, we shift how our nervous systems process threat and recovery. Neurotransmitters rebalance, cortisol levels drop, and our sense of agency returns. For some people, especially those who feel overwhelmed or shut down, movement can be the first way they reconnect to their body. It's regulation from the inside out. We might not always be able to *think* our way into calm, but we can sometimes *move* our way there. When our approach to movement is shaped by care, not control, the mental health benefits deepen. We don't have to grit our way into healing. We can dance, walk, stretch, and breathe and let movement become a place of repair, which can help our relationship with exercise be more sustainable.

Fun doesn't make something less serious or less worthwhile. In fact, the research is clear: what keeps people moving long-term isn't discipline, it's meaningful, enjoyable engagement. Joy, vitality, and connection are not just outcomes of movement; they're also the fuel that keeps us going. Positive emotions support consistency and resilience. In positive psychology, the value of positive emotions, like joy, is not only that it feels good (though that matters!) but that it broadens our thinking, helps us access more creative and flexible responses to life, and builds emotional strength and resilience over time.

That's why the kind of movement that "counts" isn't limited to structured workouts. Gardening, dancing, walking, paddleboarding, kayaking, stretching, taking the kids to the park, even doing yardwork; if it reconnects you with your body and brings you joy, it counts. These activities often go unrecognized because they don't look like punishment or productivity, but that's the point, they're based on something else. Expanding our definition of exercise and recalibrating for joy, we lose nothing and gain so much. Joy thrives when we expand the possibilities, and our sense of self expands when we value our own joy.

FROM JUDGMENT TO CURIOSITY

As we've explored throughout this section, self-compassion is the soil in which sustainable motivation grows. One of its key components, as self-compassion researcher Kristen Neff describes, is curiosity. Curiosity is a quiet act of rebellion against shame and perfectionism. It gently replaces the inner critic with a question: What would it feel like to try this differently?

Curiosity can also be the foundation of joy. When we approach movement as something to *explore* rather than something to *get right*, we give ourselves permission to enjoy it, and to learn from it, whether we liked a particular activity or not.

We can experiment with different rhythms, environments, and sensations. We can follow what feels good and let that shape our relationship. Try approaching movement as a season of gentle experimentation. There's no right answer, there's just your body, your life, and your evolving sense of what supports you and what feels good. Some days you'll try something and love it. Some days you won't. Some things you'll enjoy and others less-so, but *that's not failure*, it's feedback. And of course, the old beliefs *will* pop up. The idea that only certain kinds of movement count, beliefs about intensity, body control, etc. The voice that says you have to earn your rest or prove your worth. When they arise, you can meet them kindly, as an opportunity to practice a new self-compassionate response. Then we have space to invite something else in.

EXPLORING YOUR EXERCISE STYLE

Your movement life should reflect you and be a chance to explore and express yourself. With this curiosity, it can be a bit like trying on different outfits and seeing what feels most 'you.' Ideally, we bring as much creativity and permission-giving to this process as possible and recognize that it's to be expected that it's non-linear. You can have chapters in your exercise life where you're more into one thing, then you might move on to something else.

Here are some things to explore:

- If you reflect on your life with movement, what things stand out as having been enjoyable or meaningful and do any of those things appeal to you now?
- What types of environments most appeal to you? Time in nature? Commercial gym? Dance studio? Home workouts?
- If a friend invited you to join them, which activities feel like a 'yes' or a 'maybe': Pickleball? Swimming in the lake? Pilates class? Social dancing? Hiking? CrossFit class? Yoga on the beach? Zumba? Bike ride? Ecstatic dance? Rock Climbing? Kayaking?
- Would you prefer to do exercise in a group setting? With a buddy? With a trainer/physio? Alone?
- What could be different options that could suit different energy levels, moods, and busyness levels?
- Where do you crave challenge, slowness, structure?
- Do you like music or quietness or the sounds of nature, or a good conversation?
- What sounds like a fun thing to try just as a one-off experience?

Consider creating a list you can refer to, as part of your supportive structure, so you don't have to start from scratch every time, or consider creating a collage or other visual reminder. Make a list of 2 or 3 things you might like to try with as little expectation as possible. With the various pressures around us, we often lose sight of our own preferences. Release the expectation of finding your 'one thing' exercise style and embrace trying things on.

Orient toward what intrigues you, what would feel like a gentle or fun way to begin. Your exercise experimentation chapter can be eclectic, intuitive and seasonal, and you don't need to make it your whole identity (i.e. identifying as a runner, a yogi, or a lifter), and in fact, it may be wiser not to. Your style is whatever supports you in feeling alive!

WHAT THIS ALL ADDS UP TO

If the earlier chapters in this section helped you loosen the grip of guilt, perfectionism, and control, let this chapter remind you that joy can be the starting point, not just the destination. Joy isn't a sign you're doing it wrong; it's often a sign you're doing it *right for you*. It's not something you have to earn by getting good at something; you can start there and let it guide you forward. You're not just changing your habits or gathering up your willpower; you're reshaping your relationship with movement towards one grounded in curiosity, kindness, and attunement. That's what prepares us for what comes next: *returning to the body itself* as a home to come back to.

Part Three

Returning to
the body

*Reconnecting with a body that's
been a battleground*

CHAPTER 9

The body as self, not object

By now, you've begun to untangle your relationship with movement from the shame, pressure, and performance standards that once shaped it. You've experimented with self-compassion, explored motivation beyond discipline, and maybe even started to rediscover joy. But underneath all of this lies a deeper invitation: to return to the body not as a project to manage, but as a part of *you*, a source of knowing, expression, and connection. For many of us, this isn't easy. The world has taught us to treat our bodies like objects: to sculpt, fix, measure, or control them. But your body is not an object, it is not a machine, and it is not separate from who you are. It is the ground of your experience and existence, the home you live from. And rebuilding that relationship is one of the most powerful, tender, and transformative parts of this journey.

What we'll be exploring in this section is the shift from separation and concern about the body toward reconnection, trust, and presence to begin inhabiting the body again after perhaps decades of disconnection, fear, and chronic critique. The first port of call, lies in the subject object distinction, where we begin to practice moving from external gaze towards internal presence.

RECLAIMING A RELATIONSHIP WITH THE BODY YOU LIVE FROM

Cultural messages around "no pain, no gain," "getting your body back," or "transform your body" abound in the fitness world, and they all encourage us to *act upon* the body, reducing it to object or image and separating us from our lived experience. What we'd like to cultivate is a more embodied experience or more positive experiences of embodiment. Positive embodiment is not a look; it's a felt way of being, of living *from* the body, being attuned to, expressing from, and grounded in the physical self. This shift is foundational not only in how we move, but also in how we *exist* within ourselves. Research, including my own contributions to the literature, has shown that positive embodiment is essentially synonymous with embodied wellbeing, correlating with all dimensions of psychological wellbeing, subjective wellbeing (how positively we rate our life overall), with self-compassion, positive mood, and how we self-care and nourish ourselves. It includes how we exercise, *and it is so much more* than that. Movement and exercise have the potential to be an accessible pathway to the development of more positive experiences of embodiment, which can impact our entire lives.

As previously introduced, the Developmental Theory of Embodiment research founded by Niva Piran and colleagues iterates that we are not born disembodied; we are taught it over time by social context and life experiences, and we can learn our way back to more connection. The disconnection you may feel is not a personal failing; it's the most likely outcome of the pressures around us. The movement we engage in can either further reinforce this disconnection or it can support reconnection. For example, the same activity can have a different relationship – running can be about punishment and control or burning calories, or it can be an expression of freedom, emotional release, and expression. Our embodiment isn't good or bad; it's continually negotiated in ongoing, meaning-making processes. This is great news because it gives us space to explore and create new meaning-making experiences for ourselves. When we change the goal from sculpting or managing the body, to actually *being present* in the body, a lot can change.

WHAT DISRUPTS EMBODIMENT?

Let's walk through some of the key components from the Developmental Theory of Embodiment with a lens of movement and exercise, to first take stock of some of the forces at play that have disconnected us from our bodies. Then we'll be well-positioned to explore the pathways back more clearly.

Surveillance and Objectification

The vast majority of fitness spaces encourage constant evaluation in the form of mirrors, phone cameras, and even well-intentioned "form checks" which shift us towards watching ourselves from the outside. Even just having other us people around can accentuate this shift. This external gaze disrupts presence as we move for an audience and what it looks like from the outside, rather than *as* ourselves. This is further enmeshed with diet culture pressures and success having been dictated by appearance outcomes.

Loss of Agency and Physical Freedom

When the focus is on rigid rules, all-or-nothing plans, and tightly prescribed plans, our self-determination is limited. Like our discussion of external yardsticks, success or failure is now outside of ourselves, and the body becomes something that must submit to the plan, rather than part of ourselves that we collaborate with.

Disconnection from Bodily Cues

Oftentimes we are expected to push through fatigue, ignore our pain, and override our physiological needs in pursuit of the 'results' we are after. Hand-in-hand with our physiological hunger, we lose trust in the body's ability to sense what we need and we can even lose much of our ability to feel what we feel.

Silencing of Voice and Expression

Exercise as typically offered is rarely framed as expressive or creative unless you're a dancer or performer, and even in those cases, 'serious' creatives prioritize excellence over personal expression. We stop seeing movement as something that can be ours and an expressive outlet full of joy, creativity, and play.

Shame and Trauma

Body shame can tend to lead to either exercise avoidance or over-control in an attempt to 'fix the problem'. Trauma can make returning to the body feel unsafe and overwhelming, if that's part of your story, it's worth specialised support to unpack as part of your personal journey.

For all these reasons, and the other barriers previously discussed, embodiment can feel hard, *and that makes sense*. None of these disconnections are flaws; they've been adaptive responses to the real conditions around you. Let's turn our attention now to some of the pathways back to embodiment and how that can be explored in your exercise relationship.

PATHWAYS BACK TO EMBODIMENT

The practice of returning to the body is more about recognizing possibilities than adhering to specific prescriptions. The key is that there is agency to explore, choices to consider, and hope in cultivating something different than the status quo. These pathways can also be explored through the lens of the developmental theory of embodiment and the themes explored with the collected narratives of participants in Niva Piran and colleagues' research.

Body Connection

In our movement endeavors, we can open the invitation to practice attunement by noticing our sensations, feelings, and internal cues of what we need or want. We can develop interoceptive awareness through gentle, present movement, and a sense of curiosity and exploration within a zone of comfort. We can begin to value our physical comfort, pleasure in movement, and our safety, as a practice of shifting away from outcome and intensity orientations.

Agency

Choose how, when, and why you move. Continue the process of unraveling the layers of motivation, expectation, and "should" in your exercise process, not as something that must be all figured out but as part of the process of having a relationship to exercise and attuning to the body. Accept the notions of "should" that emerge with self-compassion, meet those critical sides of yourself with kindness and practice asking, "What do I want or need right now?" Being the expert of your own body based on your lived experience is an act of embodiment. Reconnecting to exercise in a way that doesn't have all the baggage society wants us to have is a radical act, as is claiming our strength and taking up space.

Self-Expression

Explore including movement that feels creative, freeing, silly, and personal to you. Recapturing a sense of play is incredibly healing as it allows space for expression in things you're not already 'good at.' Movement can be an act of saying 'this is me' and exploring from that space.

Relational Connection

Exercise can be social, communal, and co-regulating. Whether going on a walk with a friend, exploring group classes, or getting movement in environments where there are people around, including other people can be supportive and increase the wellbeing benefits of what you're doing. In an optimal world, choosing the spaces where you are really seen and supported can be tremendously helpful for reclaiming embodiment. Our experiences of embodiment are not only internal to us, but are also relational and political, and if these can also be aligned, the possibilities expand. Having even a single ally and friend who is on a similar path of resisting normative fitness culture and reclaiming attunement can be transformational.

Resistance and Resilience

Reclaiming strength, joy, and agency in movement is a form of healing and also an act of resistance. Exercising in a way that centres your needs is an embodied act of rejecting the systems of oppression that want us to stay small and quiet. This helps us be more resilient to these forces as they continue to swirl around us. Even small embodied acts can be subversive and powerful.

ATTUNEMENT OVER ACHIEVEMENT

With this orientation towards attunement, movement can be a conversation rather than a command. A conversation with the body over time, that grows as changes as you inevitably do too.

Exercise is a wonderful avenue to practice the skill of listening inward, adapting, and adjusting. We can give ourselves permission to explore and also permission to change course as needed; these one percent course corrections toward a more aligned and embodied way of being. We are shifting from a focus on performance and outcomes toward *process and presence*.

Embodiment isn't a one-time insight; it's a repeated choice or an orientation towards a larger vision. Here are some practical ways to explore some of these themes in daily movement. Explore the mentality of being fully fed before and after exercise, and notice any internal messaging that still tries to connect food mentality to exercise. Move without mirrors on occasion, explore not having devices or trackers, and note how things feel to you. Create a playlist you enjoy and have opportunities to move without a plan. Invite times where movement can be slow, soft, or spontaneous, not always goal oriented, and explore the 'right sizing' of structure for the moment. When discomfort or avoidance arises, this is part of the process and an invitation to explore in that direction. You may also consider exploring physical practices that support safety in the body, sensory strategies, grounding, neuro exercise, breathing with movement, gentle swaying or soothing movements. You're allowed to take your time, stay within the window of what feels good, and not have to 'get it right' on the first go. You can start small, and likely will not 'feel embodied' all the time. We're not here for a new form of perfectionism; it's about gradually building a relationship of self-trust and presence, one moment and choice at a time.

YOU ARE NOT AN OBJECT, YOU ARE THE SUBJECT OF YOUR OWN LIFE

Your body is not a thing to fix; your body is your existence, your physicality in the world and the source of your presence and power in the world. This orientation marks a turning point, shifting from managing it to establishing a resonant relationship between the self and the body. In our next chapter, we'll continue this reclamation work by addressing some areas of resistance that can be challenging, including working through fear and dealing with setbacks.

CHAPTER 10

Moving through fear: pain, injury, and the unknown

So far, we've been steadily disentangling from old stories, narratives that framed exercise as punishment, bodies as objects, and our worth as something to earn. But for many of us, the challenge isn't just in rewriting the narrative; it's in facing the quieter, deeper barriers that live in the body itself. Pain, injury, trauma, and disconnection all shape how safe it feels to move, and that safety can't be willed into place. This fear actually doesn't mean you're broken; it means your body has a lot of wisdom. If you've ever felt afraid to move, afraid of hurting yourself again, or unsure how to reconnect after a long pause or a painful experience, this chapter is for you. Fear means your body has been trying to protect you, which is something to honour, not override. We'll begin to explore what it means to move with fear in the system, rather than ignoring it, and how to start rebuilding trust from the inside out. We'll also examine why compassion and curiosity are the keys to reclaiming movement as a source of support, rather than stress. When I've explored the relationship to exercise with people over the years, fear is common, and can feel like a big rats' nest because it's simultaneously tangled together with the wider lenses of societal learning we've already been dismantling. Unravelling the layers means taking a look at each of the pieces.

WHAT KINDS OF FEAR ARE WE TALKING ABOUT?

A lot of things could be grouped together under the umbrella of 'fear' so let's define some of the sources of fear that people experience around exercise. There can be fear of pain or injury, especially after a past injury; fear of tolerating exercise for people with chronic pain or chronic fatigue; fear due to past trauma leading to dissociation, disconnection, or shutdown of the body; fear due to the role exercise has played in a history of disordered eating; fear of doing things 'wrong' and being judged; or fear around choosing to do exercise differently from the norm, by choosing to ditch diet culture, body control, and appearance focus. What is important is to acknowledge that avoidance has been a protective strategy, and we can be tremendously self-compassionate and nurture the parts of us that feel scared.

YOUR BODY IS WISE: A NERVOUS SYSTEM LENS

One helpful way to understand the fear or overwhelm that can arise around movement, especially after pain, trauma, or disconnection, is through the lens of the *window of tolerance*. This term, coined by psychiatrist Dr. Dan Siegel, describes the range of nervous system states where we can function and feel present without becoming overwhelmed or shut down. Inside our window, we have access to regulation, clarity, and choice. Outside of it, we might move into fight-or-flight reactivity, freeze, or dissociation. For many people, especially those recovering from injury, trauma, or chronic stress, the window can be narrowed, meaning even well-intended efforts like exercise can push us outside of what feels manageable. When we approach movement through this lens, the goal shifts from pushing harder to *gently widening our window* over time, so our bodies can feel safer and more supported in the activities we do or would like to do. When returning to exercise after an injury or after a difficult period we must build safety first. You'll likely need longer periods of time to build that safety than you might prefer in order to stay very much within the zone that feels good, easy, and not activating. These fear responses to exercise aren't to be pushed through with intensity and an attitude of conquering the body. Trust is gradually built over time by respecting what feels safe, and really respecting the boundaries of the body and showing up gently. This may sound like strange language to use around exercise, but our bodies have a lot of physiological protective mechanisms that need gradual repatterning to rebuild safety. When I used to work in a physio clinic, a lot of people's injuries wouldn't be structural tissue damage, but rather a protective mechanism or spasm to part of the body that has been injured in the past. The pain and limited movement are incredibly real, despite likely quite minimal structural damage. Our nervous system is always trying to protect the body and so gradually building from the zone that feels safe and supportive can be tremendously beneficial to reconnecting to exercise.

MOVING AWAY FROM "PUSH THROUGH" CULTURE

I really strongly reject the "no pain, no gain" messaging that equates discomfort with virtue and reinforces the belief that struggle is a requirement for worthiness. While there is room for challenge and effort when navigated skillfully and chosen with autonomy, for those dealing with fear this mentality teaches us to ignore or override the body's signals, as if listening to pain is weakness rather than wisdom. For people already conditioned to distrust their bodies, this is a dangerous message that can lead to burnout, injury, or further disconnection. Encouragement of dissociation and disconnection is often baked into fitness culture, even celebrated with phrases like "leave it all on the floor," or "go until you can't feel your legs" which might be said jokingly. Still, they reveal a deeper cultural orientation: your body is something to dominate, not pay attention to. This kind of disconnection can be especially harmful for people healing from trauma or learning to reconnect with their embodied awareness. Movement should be a way back into the body, not a way out of it. For people recovering from eating disorders, this type of language can be a direct trigger. Exercise compulsions are often praised or over-looked in fitness spaces, and the pressure to always be "doing more" can reinforce disordered patterns. Recovery often involves re-learning how to relate to exercise not as a tool for control or self-punishment, but as a practice of care and connection. That healing is not supported by intensity-for-intensity's-sake messaging. Post-injury, the stakes of ignoring your body's cues are higher. Fear of re-injury or triggering pain cycles is valid and shouldn't be brushed aside.

Many people in recovery need to experiment slowly and gently, with full permission to rest or modify based on how their body responds. A "push through" culture erodes that permission and replaces it with pressure and performance. In trauma-informed contexts, we're learning that the nervous system plays a central role in how safe movement feels. For someone who's been through trauma, feeling in control, grounded, and able to make choices during movement is critical. Pushing beyond limits or disregarding body cues can recreate feelings of helplessness or threat. Movement that supports healing needs to honour autonomy and sensitivity, not override it. In short, *Less is more for a whole lot of people.* Slower, gentler, more attuned movement isn't "lesser." It's often the bravest, most skillful, and most effective path forward, especially for those learning to trust their bodies again.

EMBODIED STORIES

Nothing has been more significant for navigating the complexities of my own relationship with exercise than dealing with experiences of fear and pain. When I experienced significant pain and pelvic organ prolapse following childbirth, my identity was incredibly rocked. Not only was my career physical and physically demanding, but most of my hobbies were as well. To suddenly be confronted by not only the in-the-moment physical pain, but also to project my future ability to continue life as I'd known it was very threatening to my identity. As mentioned in the introduction, this experience pointed me in the next important area of growth: separating my identity and worth from my physical performance abilities, approaching exercise and my body in new ways, and further leaning into advocacy and support for the post-natal period and unlearning anti-fat biases, toxic fitness culture, and diet culture. It would be hard to overstate how challenging that period was, despite having more knowledge of physical rehabilitation and access to care than most. I had a lot of fear about returning to movement, fearing that I would exacerbate the problems I had experienced, while simultaneously wanting to return to movement. On the psychological side, I had to acknowledge and work with the downward spiral I was in of what this would mean for my life, career, and future. A new identity and purpose did emerge but I didn't know that at the time. In my body, I had to rebuild a lot of trust, connect with my felt-sense without ruminating on the pain, and process the identity crisis. Gentleness, learning from others' stories, and finding the right supportive, empowering professionals to learn from helped me emerge from that chapter with more connection to myself and my body rather than less.

A second major challenge I experienced was suffering a concussion and dealing with post-concussion syndrome and a cluster of chronic fatigue, pain, and health issues for a period of around 2 years. Chronic pain is the most exhausting experience of my life. While I had worked with clients with chronic pain and felt for them previously, it was an entirely new level of empathy to experience such an ongoing, life-altering challenge myself. Unpredictable symptoms reshaped my relationship with movement again. I had to stop comparing myself not only to other people, but also to myself. I had continual cycles of triggering pain flares as I over estimated my capabilities, assuming a weight was 'light enough' or a workout was 'easy enough.' I frequently overdid it and wound up with migraines that lasted days. As someone who has used exercise as a significant part of my self-care and self-regulation strategy for my entire adult life, this was another layer of challenge. I had to start from a foundation of basically zero. After many false starts, the process of becoming more attuned, responsive, and adopting a wider variety of self-care strategies allowed me to return to a level of fitness that I appreciate more than I ever could have had I not experienced these struggles. It was also a powerful reminder that we do not have complete control over our physicality: we never know the struggles we may be faced with, and finding self-care and self-compassion for an embodied experience we did not expect, whether chronic illness, disability, or eventually our own physiological decline. We want to ignore these possibilities, but great freedom comes from accepting the limitations that come from living in a finite and vulnerable body.

Plenty of clients I've worked with have felt the fear around unsubscribing to diet culture. Even with subclinical degrees of disordered eating, exercise can be wrapped up with fears of weight gain and attempts to control the body. It's often worth initially separating the two to untangle the connection between activity and eating, but ultimately know these embodied experiences are connected and the layers of control, internalized fat-phobia, and personal and cultural baggage are worth lovingly unpacking to create space to move from care instead of control. I remember speaking with someone recovering from disordered eating whose therapist had been encouraging them to start exercising again for the health benefits but they were afraid of the slippery slope of compulsive exercise that had been part of their disordered experience. Firstly, like everyone, they have unconditional permission to never exercise again if they don't want to and there is no shame *and* if they did want to explore the possibilities, we talked about ways to approach that feel less threatening, such as outdoor exercise which has neither mirrors nor scales, not using exercise trackers, covering up the cardio machine displays that tell calories burned, short yoga or dance videos without body shaping messages, etc.

These examples may or may not capture *your* truth, but the hope is it normalizes some of the complexities of exercise and fear, and provides hope that if exercise is something you want to do, you can navigate the tension between that desire and the feeling of "not ready" in gentle ways, within a window of tolerance that is responsive and builds self-connection and trust.

REBUILDING A COMPASSIONATE RELATIONSHIP WITH MOVEMENT

Feeling scared and making the choice to go slowly is a sign of wisdom. Your body and mind are responding this way for a reason, and you can explore what would help you feel safe and your body to feel supported. This process takes time, experimentation, and attunement. As I shared above in my own story, setbacks can and do happen. With a more attuned approach, the setbacks can become smaller and the wins come from building self-trust rather than attaining specific outcomes. The challenges we face can become the greatest catalysts for more deeply exploring our relationships to our physical abilities, identity, and vulnerability as human beings. Not to glamourize the struggle or pain in any way, I'd willingly have skipped my own pain experiences, but if those struggles are in the mix anyway, it can be helpful to know that there are opportunities for growth in addition to the hard side. It can be both.

PRACTICAL INVITATIONS:

In the spirit of gentle and curious exploration, here are a few potential places to start. Consider something like a *Window of Tolerance journal* as a practical point to do a self check-in and notice how you feel and begin to notice what helps most at different places of tolerance. For example, on a high-pain day, this may look like only restorative practices, very light and doable movement for low-pain days, and experimenting with somewhat more moderate movement on pain-free or closer to pain-free days that doesn't trigger symptoms. Create your *own movement rating scale* with a check-in before/during/after movement to rate from 1-10 how you feel in terms of energy, comfort, and safety in your body. This could be another jot note style practice or just organically in your own mind. If it feels safe enough, a *body scan with a movement lens* is an option to ask yourself what kinds of movement feel appealing or safe on a given day. For example, ask yourself, 'Do I feel up for a short walk?' (or short workout or rehab exercises, etc) Then, scan the body to assess how that might feel and choose to stay within the range that feels accepted by your whole body. Aligned with a strategy mentioned in previous strategies, you could also consider the approach of *tiny movement experiments*. For example, getting on a mat and doing 2 mins of basic core stability and just noticing how that feels and how you want to move, or 'can I try a 5-minute walk and see how I feel?' etc.

Movement can become a source of safety and regulation in the body, and not just risk. Your body is asking to be met with care and is not broken for feeling fear. As the adage goes, slow is smooth and smooth is fast. You're allowed to go slowly, take the time to build trust, work through setbacks and flares as they emerge, and navigate this path with compassion. Becoming familiar with the patterns of fear and avoidance points us in the direction of the things that can help us feel more grounded. Respecting your current window of tolerance and allowing your journey to be different from other people or even from yourself in a previous chapter is the path of greatest self-learning and growth. This path of attunement is absolutely still for you even when and maybe even especially when the path has been fraught. This is a journey of no longer trying to conquer the body but beginning to partner with the body you actually live in at this moment, fear and all.

CHAPTER 11

Progress is not a straight line

We have been laying the foundation for a very different kind of relationship with exercise than is generally modelled for us. One that's rooted in self-compassion, aligned motivation, attunement, and embodied growth. We've started to let go of control and perfectionism and begun to imagine what it might feel like to move from a place of connection rather than pressure.

But even with all of that groundwork, there's one truth we can't skip over: life will interrupt you. Illness, travel, fatigue, stress, grief, dips in motivation, weather, hormonal fluctuations, caregiving - the list goes on: interruptions are inevitable. They don't mean you've failed; they're part of the landscape of real life and being a human being.

This chapter is about reframing what we think of as "progress" even within our new version of exercise. We're going to explore what it means to grow in ways that aren't always visible on the surface, and what deeper signs of progress could be;

things like peace, vitality, and a willingness to return, again and again, to things that feel nourishing, flexible, and supportive.

PROGRESS WITHOUT PERFECTION

It's likely quite obvious by this point that we're moving away from the idea that success is about rigidity and relentless progress. What we need to focus on is room for our humanity, with the messy, complex human-lives we actually live in. Our relationship to exercise needs resilience. The ability to move through different challenges and still allow grace. We know fitness culture likes to measure progress with metrics like numbers, workout frequency, weight, and body change, so it's no wonder that when we say "I was doing so well…" usually means "I was being consistent in a way I could measure." It makes sense. AND this measurement of doing well can collapse under pressure, then life gets in the way, and then guilt or shame enters the picture.

The truth about interruptions is that they're not failures; they're part of the process. We need to normalize these life rhythms. Here's the kicker: a compassionate response to the interruption *is the moment of growth*. Our self-trust deepens when we return, not when we never leave. A dear friend said to me, "Will your book talk about what to do when we know better but we still aren't doing it?" meaning they knew the value of exercise for themselves but currently weren't making it a 'priority.' My first thought was one of immense compassion for the self-judgment inherent in the framing of this 'problem' and for clearly seeing the tremendous period of stress, uncertainty, and demand my dear friend had been going through. Even those of us who completely *know* what exercise gives us will have periods of not doing it. The start point is to normalize it, not judge ourselves for it, and in a compassionate voice, ask ourselves what small start point could be a path back in.

A NEW DEFINITION OF PROGRESS

Progress is not about doing more or being more consistent; it's a deepening of the relationship we have with movement and our bodies.. Progress is feeling more trust in your body, more capacity to attune and adjust, more emotional regulation and fewer shame spirals, and a felt sense of agency, peace with the body, and vitality in the connection to self. A felt connection of *aliveness* and internal coherence, known as *resonance,* is a more sustainable and honest metric than any sets and reps could be. Consistency, in turn, is not about frequency or perfect schedules but about a willingness to return, to stay in a relationship with your embodied self, to be responsive to your needs over time, like a long friendship that may have gaps but can be picked back up effortlessly when you do reconnect.

The inner judgement that we have about physical activities and our consistency should be like other hobbies and things we've enjoyed that we may not always be doing. I notice a parallel with playing music or crafting. People will mention they'd like to get back to these things because they enjoy them, and they add to life and when they're included more regularly, they have value but when they aren't there's not the same level of shame as there is about not being as consistent with exercise. This degree of desiring to include more of something you like, but also not feeling the other additional layers of guilt on top, is potentially something to orient towards.

When we redefine progress as an internal landscape, we have a lot more resilience built in and can celebrate the emotional wins like showing up with less dread, enjoying a walk or maybe a strength workout, and moving with less self-monitoring. We can shift from "How many times did I make it to the gym this month?" to "How have I been feeling in my body this month?" The biggest wins are when we shift from control to more curiosity, from avoidance to experimentation, and from short-term intensity to long-term attunement. A resilient relationship to exercise is more about how you meet the challenges and interruptions than not having them. We also have to let our relationship with exercise shift and change through our lifespan and be willing to start again and have things be different. If I set myself the expectation of working out how I did as a 24-year-old without a family and with a flexible job, I am setting myself up for failure. A resilient relationship is one that evolves as you do.

A LIFE IN MOTION

If you haven't been active in months or years, you are not behind. Embodiment is a life-long journey and attunement doesn't have a clock. You're allowed a soft entry at any point. You're free to envision what suits your right now body, right now life, and right now self. Like every relationship, exercise and movement have their own rhythms and cycles, and like all paths of growth, it's a spiral, not a straight-ahead path. You're never "back at the beginning," you are further along for what you've learned. Progress isn't what it looks like from the outside, but how it feels to live as your embodied self.

Part Four

Practicing what is possible

Embodying attunement

CHAPTER 12

You are the expert of you

Embodiment is not about "doing it right" but being attuned to your body as it is in the life you are in. We've been laying the groundwork to understand how exercise has the potential to be so much more than what we do to our bodies, but a pathway of embodied agency, creativity, and integration. Being attuned is not a new type of perfection to aim for but about staying in dialogue with your body as an integral part of yourself. Every step along the way comes with opportunities to trust yourself. Perhaps one of the most critical shifts is moving from outsourcing authority to connecting with your own inner wisdom. Your own connection to your own signals is what matters, not what fitness culture, diet culture, or even what I think as the author of this book.

You are the expert of you, and when you're able to connect with your own body, explore with curiosity and notice your own feedback loops, you're reclaiming your agency from systems that teach you to distrust, override and control your body. Whatever you do or don't do, enjoy or don't enjoy, becomes feedback and a source of insight in an ongoing conversation. Beginning to explore, with maybe a flexible workout plan, or trying a class, or setting an intention to take a few walks, is a good way to start knowing yourself more deeply. If you did it, great! Notice how you feel mentally, how your body feels, and what thoughts go with that. If you didn't do it, great! Notice how you feel mentally, how your body feels, and what thoughts go with that. This is an iterative process and a lifelong journey. That orientation is what helps us not get stuck in the mire of shame and guilt. Of course, those thoughts will come up, which again provides the opportunity to meet them with compassion and nurturing.

Your journey with attuned exercise might not look like any-one else's, and chances are it won't look the same a few years in (or a lot of years in!) as it does when you first invite this new way of relating into your life. This is because you have the final word. You can utilize structure, workout plans, or guidance from professionals where it suits you, or you can reject all of that entirely. This is a self-led process where it's not about one right method but creating a resonant, connected relationship with your embodied self. It could be useful to periodically check in, 'Does what I'm doing support my energy, values, and needs right now? Are there ways I can adapt and personalize it?' This is a living dialogue, each day or life chapter may come with different cues, like fatigue, enthusiasm, dread, joy, soreness, curiosity. The more you practice tuning in, the more fluent the dialogue is, and this increased attunement builds trust and, in turn, sustainability.

THE BODY IN HEALING

The practices of attuning, being compassionate, noticing emotions and sensations in the body and unpacking social and cultural pressures we've absorbed are a route to a more positive and energy-giving relationship with exercise *and also* this relationship with exercise can be a gentle, embodied route to reconnect with your whole self in a more integrated way. In the psychology and psychotherapy world in recent times, there has been a growing interest in including the body more in the healing journey in therapy settings. Flipping that dynamic on its head and letting movement and exercise itself be the starting point as a space to practice listening to the body, meeting oneself with compassion, and learning how to dismantle social beliefs has the potential to be incredibly healing. For those navigating illness, trauma, or disconnection, exercise and movement approached with care can be powerful. Movement of course, does not take the place of other therapeutic modalities; these are necessary for many people's growth journeys. The point is that healing can happen through the body and through our embodied experiences and choices, we can reclaim movement as safe, connected, and also powerful, which can extend far beyond the time in the gym.

Not only can you have a relationship with exercise that doesn't have the negative aspects of shame, body control, and health-based fears, but you can have one that is *so much more*. One that provides an arena to practice self-compassion, values your agency and expression, listens to the body for safety cues, and allows you to embody your power, strength, and even your vulnerabilities. It's a pathway into the body that's way more accessible to most people than a 'where do you feel that in your body?' tossed into the middle of a conversation. It's a practice of being your own top authority from your felt-sensations, re-claiming your voice and making it your own.

What begins as movement can ripple outward into how we relate to the rest of our lives. This isn't *just about* exercise anymore, but about the kind of relationship you want with yourself and with the world. This embodied dialogue doesn't stay confined to workouts or walks; it can change how we make decisions, how we show up, and how we live in our own bod-ies. The body, once treated as a project or problem, becomes a partner in movement and in life. When we move from control into connection, we begin to inhabit our lives differently. In the next chapter, we'll explore how this relationship with your body becomes a foundation not just for exercise, but for a more pres-ent, more integrated life. Attunement doesn't stay in the gym; it moves with you, into the way you live, feel, and connect.

CHAPTER 13

The embodied self: beyond the gym and into your life

Just as your body isn't just something you *have,* it's also something you *are;* exercise is not just something you *do,* it is *a way of being.* How you relate to your body through exercise is connected to your emotions, your inner life, and much wider dynamics. What we'll explore in this chapter is not just the possibility of a relationship with exercise that is more in sync, but also the possibility of a life that is more in sync. Beyond adopting a new set of habits lies the possibility of a felt reality of integration, where your body is *not separate* from your mind, life, and self.

EMBODIED PRESENCE

When the body is no longer a battleground, it can be a resource, the source of your presence in your own life, and the foundation of a regulated way of being. Your body isn't just where stress shows up; it can also be the place where safety can grow. Exploring exercise and reclaiming movement and physicality helps build tolerance for feeling, noticing, and recovering. We expand the window of tolerance when we have a wide variety of supporting and regulating options. Simple practices, such as walking when we feel overwhelmed, noticing tension patterns and meeting them compassionately, and feeling grounded and supported in the body, can all be part of the mix. We can practice aligned self-care, embodying agency, and feeling our own physical self-efficacy. Embodied presence is a form of self-trust that can be explored during exercise when we feel like we can be fully present with our whole selves. Not just 'letting off steam' or escaping life through sports, but being grounded and present through physical practices. I'm aware this is way beyond the generally talked about benefits of exercise for health and fitness, but because it is something we are doing with the body, why not explore the possibilities that may emerge when we truly are *with* our bodies?

AUTHENTICITY AND EMBODIMENT

There is more to authenticity than platitudes of 'be yourself.' While much focus is on the congruence of what's on the inside and what is expressed, most of us who wish for more authenticity would benefit from a deeper awareness of our own inner dynamics. Essentially, most of us aren't trying to be hypocrites; there's just more going on under the surface than we're aware of. A greater understanding of our actual physiological sensations, emotional patterns, and dynamics helps us be in greater alignment with ourselves internally; from there, the outer actions flow naturally. Embodiment builds the awareness of these internal dynamics, which isn't about getting it all right, but about increasing our capacity to notice and, in turn, act from that place. We must know ourselves before we can live with authenticity, and it is very hard to know ourselves if we are alienated from our physiological self. The opposite of alienation, according to sociologist Hartmut Rosa, is resonance. When your body and inner world are in dialogue, your capacity to be in resonant, meaningful relationships with others, the world, and the work that matters to you also has the potential to increase. Resonant relationships to the world are essential to creating positive change because we need to feel that, as the world moves us, we can also move the world and express agency and self-efficacy. The world needs embodied leaders, communities need embodied care, and you deserve an embodied life.

GROWTH AND RESONANCE

Far from being standard-issue self-improvement, what the foundation of self-compassion offers is growth that happens organically and in a grounded way. In that way, embodiment is not a place to strive for, it is emergent and more of a homecoming than a new place to strive for. The physical activities you explore are spaces you can show up as you are, sometimes soft, sometimes strong, at times inconsistent, but alive. We're reclaiming what socialization took, our sense of play, joy, agency, and worthiness, just as you are. Growth is not about achievement but your growing capacity to be present. The more attuned you are, the more your capacity for resonance grows, and it starts with your own relationship with your body. Exercise is the *arena for practicing a more resonant life and can teach us how to feel, respond, be moved,* and move with intention.

A LIFE FOR YOU

None of this is a destination; it's a way of being and a practice of returning. Your body is not a barrier to be overcome; it is the bridge to possibility. Attunement deepens over time, not by getting it all down pat, but by staying close to yourself as you go. The work of being a body, with care and often courage, is the work of becoming a person.

Acknowledgments

First and foremost, to all the people who have trusted me in your journey with exercise over the years. Those who came to classes, workshops, personal training, coaching or Pilates appointments and trusted me with your stories of struggle and resilience: this book is for you. Thank you for allowing me to witness your courage, your vulnerability, and your strength. You are the living proof that a different relationship with exercise is possible.

This book could not have come into being without the support, wisdom, and presence of so many people who have walked alongside me. Writing is often a solitary process, but this one has felt supported, encouraged, and inspired by a community.

To my Book Doula and publisher, Andrea Seydel, thank you for believing in this project from the very beginning, for helping me shape these ideas into their clearest form, for resonating so strongly with the ethos of the book and its purpose, and for guiding me through the process of bringing a book into the world.

To the mentors and teachers whose paths have crossed mine, including Louisa Jewell, who first encouraged me to pursue a masters in positive psychology and go deeper about positive psychology and the body; Jessie Mundell whose perspective on not only post-natal fitness but a more radical perspective of exercise came along at a crucial juncture and led me down a path of thinking much bigger about exercise; and the instructors at the University of East London in the MAPPCP program and Sarah Woodruff at the Human Kinetics department at the University of Windsor for always encouraging my journey into research. To the teachers, researchers, and communities whose work laid the groundwork for this book, including Niva Piran, Tanya Teall, Catherine Cook-Cottone, and other embodiment researchers, your research created the scaffolding that allowed these concepts to take shape. I am grateful for the many books, podcasts and researchers whose conversations and insights expanded my thinking and inspired me to stay connected to the heart of what I wanted to say.

To my family and friends, thank you for your patience, love, and constant presence through the writing process and my life more generally. To Vainatey, thank you for grounding me, for providing the support I needed to pursue my Master's, my research projects, and now this book, and for honestly being the best partner I could ask for. To Nisha, for being the inspiration to create a better world in the future. To Galina and Reesa, for being my very first readers and forever cheerleaders.

I also hold deep gratitude for you, dear reader. I hope these words carry you, allow you to see possibilities, and trust in yourself.

Thank you.

Walking through a few examples

Throughout the book, I've avoided giving overly specific workout programs. That's because I wanted the core concepts to feel open and adaptable, rather than prescriptive about what your exercise life *should* look like. That said, I know it can be helpful to see a few examples of how I might approach working with people at different stages of their Attuned Exercise journey.

Example 1: A complete beginner
Not currently exercising, minimal experience, has received medical clearance to begin.

For those experiencing major limitations. such as disabilities, chronic illness or pain, past injuries or surgeries, I'd recommend starting with a physiotherapy assessment and incorporating the suggested exercises as a foundation.

At the same time, I'd encourage beginning a reflective practice alongside the physical work. This could be journaling or using prompts from this book to explore your relationship with exercise as you go.

The initial goal here is simple: stay curious. Begin exploring both structured and unstructured movement. Less-structured options could include dancing, outdoor activities, social walks, or other playful, everyday movements. For structured exercise, explore what feels accessible: community classes, gyms, online videos, or home workouts.

When starting, I usually suggest keeping intensity moderate (around a 6–ish out of 10 in perceived effort). This helps build confidence, avoids excessive soreness, and keeps the experience positive. If I were guiding someone through this stage with home workouts, I'd design a flexible program (see example later) while also encouraging them to incorporate unstructured movement opportunities into their daily life.

Example 2: Already exercising, but struggling with motivation
Currently showing up inconsistently, unpacking diet culture beliefs, and in the stage of "wanting to want to exercise."

Here, the initial focus is on self-compassion and unlearning. Many people in this stage are carrying beliefs shaped by diet culture. Resources like *Anti-Diet* by Christy Harrison or *Body Trust* by Hilary Kinavey can be valuable companions, as can podcasts or social media accounts that challenge diet mentality.

The next step is to practice connecting more deeply to the body while moving. This could involve creating a visual map of your relationship with exercise, noticing patterns of thought during workouts, and holding those thoughts with compassion rather than judgment.

On a practical level, it helps to:

- Experiment with different intensities and notice how they feel.

- Rate exercise on a 1–10 scale and track what you enjoy vs. don't enjoy.
- Use flexible programming (see example later).
- Practice auto-regulation, adjusting workouts in the moment based on how you feel. This could mean scaling intensity, modifying movements, or practicing self-advocacy and agency in a group class setting.

The long-term focus here is to build self-efficacy: the belief that you can always return to exercise when the time is right. Over time, this fosters self-trust, helps you let go of all-or-nothing beliefs, and makes room for attunement.

Example 3: Already active, mostly positive relationship

Regularly exercising, no longer driven by control, but still experiences challenges from time to time.

Hey, look at you! You've made it this far! It might not feel "perfect," but that's completely okay. This is a lifelong journey, and it's natural for things to pop up along the way.

When challenges do arise, try to notice what else is happening in life. In my experience, how we feel about exercise often mirrors other dynamics:

When we feel pressure to hustle in workouts, there may be hustle showing up in other areas.

When body-related thoughts get louder, there may be vulnerability across other domains of life.

When motivation dips, it often reflects being over-taxed elsewhere.

Looking at the bigger picture helps us move through the natural ebbs and flows of exercise, life, and our ever-changing bodies.

At this stage, it can be powerful to reflect back on your lifetime journey with movement; acknowledge the sticky spots but also celebrate how far you've come. The opportunity now is to notice how attunement, body awareness, self-trust, and self-compassion practiced in exercise can overflow into the rest of your life. Lean into learning more if that resonates (ie, books or podcasts) and don't underestimate the power of connection and finding communities, or even one person to share this journey with can be a game-changer.

I like the axiom "everything is everything." The way we orient ourselves in one area, like perfectionism or self-kindness, often reflects how we show up elsewhere. The skills you've built here, such as self-efficacy or resisting outside measures of success, can ripple outward into other domains of life as well. The biggest possible picture is a good place to check in with regularly.

APPENDIX 2:

Flexible, stackable workout plan example

One of the most common sticking points for getting started is the tension between wanting some structure but not wanting it to become rigid, overwhelming, or unsustainable. A stackable, modular approach is one way to ease that tension. Instead of a fixed plan you have to follow no matter what, you create small building blocks of movement that can stand alone or be combined depending on your energy, time, and mood. This way, every option "counts," and you always have a way to engage with your body without falling into the all-or-nothing trap.

Intention: To get some movement and notice how you feel during and after. (After receiving medical clearance and instruction on any exercises you don't yet have confidence with)

Effort: aim for ~6/10 to start with. Err on the side of less rather than more.

Breathing cue: 6–7/10 is the point where you may start mouth-breathing. Staying under 7 keeps you with nose-breathing, which can be a physical cue to begin to notice.

Focus: quality, ease, curiosity about how you feel rather than intensity or pushing through.

HOW THIS PLAN WORKS

There are **Chunks** you can use alone or stack together depending on your energy, preferences, and mood.
Each chunk lasts about 3–5 minutes.
You can do one on its own or combine several for a longer session when it feels right.
Example combos are provided at the end.

Warm-Up Chunk (choose or mix)
3–5 minutes of light movement: dancing, brisk walking, or a few gentle mat Pilates–style exercises
Include some range of motion (arm swings, hip circles), balance (standing on one leg), or eye stability drills.

Core Chunk (example)

Leg Lift Supine
- Lie on your back, knees bent, feet flat, pillow under head.
- Keep pelvis steady, lift one foot an inch off floor, hold 5 sec, return. Alternate sides.
- Start with ~10 reps, build toward 60–90 sec total.

Progression: feet placed farther from buttocks.

Bridge Supine

- Lie on back, knees bent, feet flat (minimal pillow).
- Lift hips gently without flaring ribs. Keep weight toward feet, not shoulders.
- Hold 5 sec, return.
- Start with ~10 reps, build toward 60–90 sec total.

Progression: add ball squeeze at top, then small single-leg lifts.

Prone Leg Extension

- Lie face down, forehead resting on hands.
- Reach one leg long, lift slightly (hip extension only). Hold 5 sec, switch sides.
- Start with ~10 reps, build toward 60–90 sec total.

Progression: try sphinx position, gentle eye gaze forward, later add alternating arm reach (only if no neck/shoulder tension).

Hip Abduction with Band

- Lie in bridge position, band above knees.
- Push knees out to parallel, hold 5 sec, return.
- Start with ~10 reps, build toward 60–90 sec total.

Progression: gradually heavier bands. Focus on activation, not max strength.

Hip Adduction with Ball

- Bridge position with a small ball between thighs.
- Squeeze moderately, hold 5 sec, release.
- Start with ~10 reps, build toward 60–90 sec total.

Progression: firmer squeezes, same ball.

STRENGTH PAIR CHUNK EXAMPLES

(Choose one or two pairs for variety. Each pair alternates two moves, 2–3 rounds.)

Squat Variation + Push-Up Variation

- Squat variation can range from assisted, to body weight, to goblet squat, to barbell versions appropriate to the current level of fitness and what feels good (6-7/10 effort)
- Push-up Variation may range from wall-push-ups, to bench pushups, floor pushups, or other upper body push exercises if preferred (like bench press or cable press)
- Start with ~8-10 reps if you're starting with lighter reps, if you're more experienced at higher levels of effort and enjoy those ranges explore sets of ~5

Deadlift Pattern (hip hinge) + Overhead press Variation

- Deadlift variation can include kettlebell deadlift, machine deadlift, barbell deadlift variations based on current level, comfort with the movement, and personal preference
- Shoulder Press Variation may range from dumbbell shoulder presses to machine presses, variations in position (seated or standing) and vary between single arm or both arms together
- Start with ~8-10 reps if you're starting with lighter reps, if you're more experienced at higher levels of effort and enjoy those ranges explore sets of ~5 or fewer for deadlifts especially

Lunge or step-ups (single leg) + Row Variation
- Single Leg exercises can include step-back lunges, walking lunges, step ups, or other single leg movements. You can do these assisted, with machines, using body weight, or adding dumbbells or other free weights. Choose movements you're comfortable with to get started
- Row Variation may range from cable machine, resistance bands, dumbbells or barbells
- Start with ~8-10 reps (per side for the single leg exercises) if you're starting with lighter reps, if you're more experienced at higher levels of effort and enjoy those ranges explore sets of ~5

EXAMPLE STACKS

Low Energy Day *(5–10 min):* Warm-Up + one Core Chunk.
Medium Energy Day (15–20 min): Warm-Up + Core Chunk + one Strength Pair.

High Energy Day *(25–30 min):* Warm-Up + Core Chunk + two or three Strength Pairs.

The key idea: *each "chunk" counts.* Whether you do one or many, you're building consistency and a deeper relationship with your body and practicing modifying based on attunement. You can rotate which strength pairs you focus on or choose one pair to focus on until you feel very confident with the movements. As you get stronger, it may take longer to complete the workout as suggested and can be adjusted to suit your life, preferences, and needs in whatever chapter. The ethos of including this section, in addition to the balance of structure and attunement, is also to demystify strength training a little bit for those who want to do it but may be intimidated. Don't underestimate how far a 'simple' program like this can take you. Start easy, when it feels good and strong, increase the weight little by little, and build your confidence as you go. If these exercises are unfamiliar, get some support to learn the basics of each movement, but once you're comfortable with these 6 movements, you'll be rolling.

This is just one example of how a modular approach can be practical. The details matter far less than the spirit: having a few supportive pieces you can mix and match gives you structure without rigidity, and room to respond to your actual energy, mood, and needs that day. Your version might look entirely different, but what matters is creating a toolkit that feels like it belongs to you, so movement becomes something you can return to with flexibility, curiosity, and trust.

About the author

Martha Munroe is a passionate coach and speaker who helps people get curious to grow from a place of self-compassion. Through her work as a fitness professional-turned-researcher, she has inspired countless people to reimagine what their relationship to exercise could be, foster greater self-trust, increase body acceptance, and reclaim joy in movement. She is relentlessly curious, heart-led yet research-driven, and equal parts deeply philosophical and perennially playful.

When she's not writing, Martha enjoys time outdoors, lifting heavy things, creating music, and hanging out with her family.

Connect with Martha for speaking & workshop opportunities, 1:1 coaching, and online offerings.
Visit AttunedExercise.com or MarthaMunroe.com to learn more or connect directly.

If you loved this book, please consider leaving a review or sharing it with a friend—it helps more than you know!

About the publisher

Dear Reader,

As you hold this remarkable book in your hands, we want to express our heartfelt gratitude for becoming a part of the Live Life Happy Community of readers. Your curiosity and thirst for knowledge fuel our passion for publishing meaningful non-fiction works.

At Live Life Happy Publishing, our mission is rooted in bringing forth literature that not only entertains but uplifts, supports, and nourishes the soul. We firmly believe that books have the power to transform lives, to ignite passions, and to spread joy far and wide.

Behind every word, every chapter, lies the dedication of our authors who pour their hearts and souls into their craft. Their ultimate aim? To touch your life in profound ways, to inspire, and to leave an indelible mark on your journey.

Your role in this journey is invaluable; by sharing your thoughts through reviews, spreading the word to others, or reaching out to the authors themselves, you become an integral part of sparking transformation in countless lives, igniting a ripple effect of joy and enlightenment.

And if, perchance, you or someone you know has dreams of writing, of sharing a message, or of unleashing a powerful story unto the world, know that Live Life Happy Publishing stands ready to guide you. Our doors are open, our ears attuned, and our hearts eager to hear your message.

So, dear reader, let us, continue to spread the power of literature, one page at a time. Reach out, share, and most importantly, never underestimate the power of your message to touch lives.

With warmest regards,

LiveLifeHappyPublishing.com
P.S. Remember, books change lives. Whose life will you touch with yours?

LiveLifeHappy
Publishing

www.ingramcontent.com/pod-product-compliance
Lightning Source LLC
Chambersburg PA
CBHW072124090426
42739CB00012B/3057